Fire

TIME EN(

"Yemi Ladipo provides a much-needed ...
later life who all too often have to put up with platitudes and false
promises. He writes about growing old with gritty honesty and
relaxed humour. Firmly rooted in his Christian faith, Yemi uses
stories from his own and others' experience as well as from a wealth
of scripture to reveal the potential and richness of old age. Above all,
the advice here is highly practical as well as being a book of wisdom."
George Pitcher

"Yemi Ladipo has written an immensely positive, practical,
encouraging and thought-provoking book. He warmly, winsomely,
and humbly comes alongside us as we read, drawing us in on his own
journey of discovery. He has a light touch, but packs a punch –
provoking us to face up to the challenges of retirement and our
ageing bodies. He also shows us the opportunities that both provide.
These include the opportunity to get ready for the inevitable, refocus
our priorities, do things differently, invest in people not things, and
be a blessing not a curse to those whom we will leave behind! Yemi
shows us not only how to face retirement, but how to keep on
inwardly growing through it. For those for whom this topic may be a
bit scary, Yemi doesn't hesitate to grapple with difficult issues, but
does so with gentleness and compassion."
John & Kate Arkell

"I was delighted by the book's creative and absorbing style of
presentation. Even more refreshing for me was the rich and
instructive information on preparing for and coping with the
inevitability of old age. As one who officially retired almost 18 years
ago, I thought I was experienced in managing my retirement years.
But having read Yemi's book, I now wish I had attended his seminars
long before May 2003!"
David Balogun

"By age thirty I had it all: a good education, a well-paying profession, material wealth, and a good marriage and family. But I was bored! Spurred on by this boredom I pursued meaning and purpose with earnestness in all the usual places that this world suggests they can be found. But still they alluded me! Then, in 1976 I carted my family off to Nigeria to embark on a teaching assignment. It was there that I met Yemi Ladipo, who soon after shared with me the same transformative perspective which this book so lucidly articulates."
Jim Kesselring

YEMI LADIPO

Time Enough for Life

Growing older, gracefully

FIREFINCH BOOKS
London

First published in Great Britain in 2022 by
Firefinch Books
www.firefinchbooks.com

Copyright © Yemi Ladipo 2022

The right of Yemi Ladipo to be identified as the author of this work has been asserted by him.

All rights reserved. No part of this book may be reproduced, copied, distributed or adapted in any way, with the exception of certain activities permitted by applicable copyright laws, such as brief quotations in the context of a review or academic work.

Every effort has been made to acknowledge fully the sources of material reproduced in this book. The author apologises for any omissions that may remain and, if notified, will ensure full acknowledgements are made in a subsequent edition.

ISBN: 9798797911241

DEDICATION

To my grandchildren: Julian, Oskar and Frieda.

With lots of love.

CONTENTS

	Acknowledgments	i
1	Life Gets Shorter by the Day	1
2	Retirement is a New Adventure	17
3	Deepening of Loving Relationships	48
4	Learning to Cooperate with the Inevitable	72
	Epilogue	94
	Notes	96
	About the Author	

ACKNOWLEDGMENTS

Many thanks to all those who participated in the seminar series in which I first expressed the ideas contained in this book. Your insights and feedback were invaluable. I am also indebted to John Arkell, David Balogun, Jim Kesselring, Mark Pearson, Rosie Pearson and George Pitcher for their constant encouragement and painstaking editorial efforts. Last, but not least, I am grateful to my very own 'Epictetus' for serving as my long-suffering amanuensis.

CHAPTER 1

LIFE GETS SHORTER BY THE DAY

"Everybody knows they're going to die, but no one really believes it." (Spalding Gray)[1]

I have read quite a number of books written by writers who are in, or contemplating, retirement; but only very few of them touched on three important areas of concern for me. First, the lack of 'death awareness' especially among the well to do of our society. Second, the need for those approaching retirement age to be made aware of some of the challenges and opportunities that lie ahead of them. And thirdly, the need to be aware of the challenge of dealing with a life that goes on long after the thrill of living is gone. Consequently, I was encouraged to respond to Toni Morrison's advice to budding writers: "If there's a book that you want to read, but it hasn't been written yet, then you must write it." [2]

That was why I spent the first ten years of my retirement reading as many books on the subject as I could lay hands on; while at the same time jotting down my own experience.

Death was a common experience among the community I grew up in. I was born in the city of Ibadan in Nigeria in 1937; and growing up in the '40s and '50s I was acutely aware of how privileged I was to live in a home with modern amenities such as clean running water, electricity, a fridge, mosquito nets, a radio, and a telephone.

Most of my playmates were not so fortunate. They were brought up in conditions of urban poverty and material deprivation and many of them died young from preventable diseases such as malaria and smallpox. Thus, very early in my childhood, I was conscious of the fragility of life.

However, it was the sudden death of my father at the beginning of my last year in high school that brought home to me the brevity of human life. Now, as an octogenarian, I am even more aware than ever, that life gets shorter by the day. And, in turn, this consciousness informs the core intention behind this book which is to remind my readers that life involves dealing with the certainty of the unexpected; and that for many people death is the most unexpected event of all. It is wise, particularly for the elderly, to bear this in mind in everything they do.

"The living know they will die, but the dead know nothing; they have no further reward, and even the memory of them is forgotten." (Ecclesiastes 9:5)

No one can afford to cruise through life thinking that everything is going to be just fine.

It takes only a call from the doctor telling us that

we have a life-threatening disease, or a sudden swerve of a careless driver coming towards us, to remind us that life is extremely uncertain. There are no sure guarantees. None of us can be absolutely certain of the next breath.

In the book 'Nearing Home', written by the renowned international evangelist Billy Graham (at the age of 92), the opening paragraph reads: "I never thought I would live to be this old. All my life I was taught how to die as a Christian; but no one ever taught me how I ought to live in the years before I die. I wish they had because I am an old man now, and, believe me, it is not easy. Whoever first said it was right: old age is not for sissies."[3]

Graham then goes on to exhort his readers to "enjoy life: it has an expiration date" and reminds them that "the only thing that comes to us without effort is old age".

In an article published in the Guardian on 5 October 2013, the writer Penelope Lively boldly stated that: "I am 80, so I am old, no question…[and] I have arrived at the state of death-consciousness [which accepts] that we cannot truly savour life without a regular awareness of extinction". But she also concluded her article with the following confession: "I never imagined that old age would be quite like this – possibly because, like most, I never much bothered to imagine it".[4]

So, here we have it: a well-known evangelist and a non-faith professing writer, both agreeing that they have not given the process of dying a serious thought. Death, unfortunately, is something we consign to hospitals and care homes. It is not a subject of polite conversation. And yet our lives are brief and seen by few. The American playwright, Woody Allen, once said, "I don't want to achieve immortality through my work, I want to achieve it through not dying."

This contemporary denial of mortality is shared even by those whose profession brings them into daily contact with the reality of death. A medical doctor living with terminal cancer described her feelings as being "like waiting for a train and not knowing when it would come except I am still hoping that my train will be cancelled." Such feelings are instantly recognizable to most people currently suffering from serious illness. Or, as Atul Gawande puts it in 'Letting Go': "Ninety-nine percent of hospital patients understand they're dying, but one hundred percent hope they are not. They all want to beat their disease".[5]

In 'The Living End', Dr Guy Brown, a cell biologist, writes that: "Before the advent of modern medicine those who made it to adulthood tended to die from infection, childbirth or violence. Reaching old age was exceptional. Today, the average lifespan in the developed world has reached 78 years and continues to stretch upwards at the rate of two years every decade. It is now thought that in the UK by the year 2030 there will be 4 million people who are over-80."[6]

Brown suggests that death has been transformed from a "digital", event-like, switching off, to an "analogue" process, like a dimmer switch turned down.

He also notes that while modern medicine has enabled us to delay the moment of death, it has made far less progress in tackling the effect of ageing. In his view, there is an urgent need for a complete rethink of the place of death in modern life.

Brown's views are echoed by James Wilsdon when he notes that: "Life expectancy is rising, but the number of years we expect to remain healthy isn't. Is it time to challenge the ageing process and learn how to die?".[7]

Ironically, it seems that much of the discussion about ageing is progressing in the other direction. Instead of learning how to age more gracefully and face death with more equanimity and deliberation, there is a relentless focus on the quixotic effort to "defeat" and "combat" ageing.

We are told that 100,000 people die every day world-wide from the preventable effects of old age and that Americans spend more than $20 billion annually on various anti-ageing products that claim to cure baldness, remove wrinkles, build muscle and renew powers of youth. Can those products really deliver what they promise? For longevity crusaders like Aubrey de Grey, it's simply a matter of time before modern medical science "solves" the problem of ageing. From de Grey's perspective, ageing of the body, just like the aging of a car, is merely a "preventative maintenance" problem.[8] Thus, in his vision of the future, "people receiving cell regeneration therapies would be able to constantly add more time to their lives whenever their bodies began to break down".[9]

When faced with this naive faith in the wonders of science, it is tempting to note that modern medical sciences still have a long way to go in prolonging human life if they are to match the oft-cited Biblical examples of Methuselah who died at 969 years in Genesis 5:26, or King Hezekiah (2 Kings 20:6) who was given a 15-year extension of his life; and certainly none to equal the way Jesus raised Lazarus from the dead in John 11:43.

However, at a more prosaic level, we should also remind ourselves that (to quote the words of Dr Thomas Perls of the Boston University School of Medicine) "there is absolutely no scientific proof that any commercially available product will stop or reverse ageing."[10]

In fact, rather than *solving* the problem of ageing, modern medical science may simply have *complicated* and *lengthened* the problem. As Atul Gawande puts it in 'Letting Go': "modern medicine is good at staving off death with aggressive intervention and bad at knowing when to focus, instead, on improving the days that terminal patients have left."

For a seminar series I put together before the start of the Covid-19 pandemic, I began collating a list of books which adroitly address the problem of the life that goes on long after the thrill of living is gone. The list includes the writers listed in the table overleaf.

Phillip Roth	'Everyman' and 'Patrimony'
J M Coetzee	'Slow Man'
Linda Grant	'Remind Me Who I Am, Again'
Alice La Plante	'Turn of Mind'
Julian Barnes	'Nothing to be Frightened Of'
Marilynne Robinson*	The 'Gilead' Series
David Winter*	'At the End of the Day'
George Pitcher*	'A Time to Live'
Meike Ziervogel	'Clara's Daughter'
Ian Knox*	'Finishing Well'
John Mortimer	'The Summer of a Doormouse'
Billy Graham*	'Nearing Home'
Christopher Matthews	'The Old Man and the Knee'
Simon Gray	'Coda'
Atul Gawande	'Being Mortal'
Ernest Hemingway	'The Old Man and the Sea'
Rowan Williams*	'Being Human'
Diana Athill	'Somewhere Towards the End'
Sarah Ladipo Manyika*	'Like a Mule Bringing Ice Cream to the Sun'

*These are books by professing Christian writers

For my seminar series I also compiled a selection of my favourite quotations and aphorisms on the subject of ageing and mortality. Among others, they included the following:

"I never think of the future. It comes soon enough." (Albert Einstein)[11]

"What is the most important lesson life has taught me? That it's not a rehearsal." (Jenny Agutter)[12]

"Old age is the most unexpected of all things that can happen to a man". (Leon Trotsky)[13]

"The fact of our mortality means that every project we have is limited. There is something non-negotiable about that absolute limit, and there is an ultimate challenge in that to any fantasy or fiction of the all-powerful ego." (Rowan Williams)[14]

"I think that if people began thinking about death sooner they'd make fewer mistakes" (Dmitri Shostakovich)[15]

"Few things are less distinguished than death, that most democratic of all events and the oldest of jokes that comes to each of us afresh." (Joseph Epstein)[16]

"Happy is the man who hath the hour of his death always before his eyes, and daily prepareth himself to die." (Thomas a Kempis)[17]

"Death is the destiny of everyone; the living should take this to heart." (Ecclesiastics 7:2)

In the course of compiling both these lists (of books and aphorisms) I was struck by the fact that they were penned by a curious mixture of Christians, agnostics and atheists. In other words, wisdom in the face of death appears to be as democratically distributed as death itself. Nevertheless, it is with the Biblical perspective on death (and the dying process), that I am most familiar and to which my heart keeps reverting. Indeed, I often wonder whether the lessons contained in all the contemporary books about ageing can be summed up in the words of the Psalms.

The Psalms teach us that awareness of our mortality should help us focus our energies and rebalance our priorities:

"Teach us to number our days aright, that we may apply our hearts unto wisdom." (Psalms 90:12)

"Show me O Lord, my life's end and the number of my days; let me know how fleeting my life is." (Psalm 39:4)

More explicitly, the Psalms also teach us the futility of directing our endeavours to the accumulation of wealth and social status:

"No one can redeem the life of another or give to God a ransom for him – the ransom for a life is costly, no payment is ever enough – so that he should live on forever and not see decay. For all can see that wise men die; the foolish and the senseless alike perish and leave their wealth to others." (Psalm 49:7-9)

But the Psalms also teach us other, equally important, things. For example, when faced with the reality of the ageing process, we can (like Dylan Thomas) vainly "rage against the dying of the light"[18] or we can leave the unknowable in the hands of the all-knowing God and join in praise with the Psalmist when he remembers that:

"All the days ordained for me were written in your book before one of them came to pass". Psalm 139:16

Do the Psalmist's words mean that as we enter into old age and come closer to death, we should sink into apathy and listlessness? Far from it. The important thing is not to wait in idleness but to be actively engaged in holy living in the power of the Holy Spirit and in making Christ known.

While Dylan Thomas adjures that "old age should burn and rave at close of day", the Bible says something similar but very (very) different. We should burn not with rage and resentment but in the love and light of Christ and with the determination to pass on the torch to the next generation.

"Even when I am old and grey, do not forsake me O God, till I declare your power to the next generation, your might to all who are to come." (Psalm 71:18)

"I consider my life worth nothing to me, if only I may finish the race and complete the task which the Lord has given me-the task of testifying to the gospel of God's grace." (Acts 20:24)

A good illustration of this biblical approach to the duties of old age can be found in the life of Paul, the Apostle to the Gentiles, (formally a renowned intellectual Pharisee called Saul) who became a poacher turned game-keeper as a result of his personal encounter with Christ on the road to Damascus. Arguably, of all Christ's Apostles, it is Paul who has the most to say about the ageing process and about life after death. Indeed, Paul was always keenly aware of his own mortality and, far from coasting along to heaven, Paul was firing on all cylinders to the very end.

In his letter to the Philippians (Philippians 1:20), he says: "I eagerly expect and hope that I will in no way be ashamed, but will have sufficient courage so that now as always Christ will be exalted in my body, whether by life or by death". And in the following sentence he notes that: "For to me, to live is Christ and to die is gain".

Later, towards, the end of his life, Paul writes to the Christian fellowship (in 2 Corinthians 4:16-18) to assure them he is not losing heart and to remind them that: "Though outwardly we are wasting away, yet inwardly we are being renewed day by day. For our light and momentary troubles are achieving for us an eternal glory that far outweighs them all. So, we fix our eyes not on what is seen, but on what is unseen. For what is seen is temporary, but what is unseen is eternal."

What Paul is saying in these verses is two-fold. Firstly, that a Christian understanding of the meaning of life on planet earth or life after death stems from a personal experience of the living God through Christ. Secondly, that death is not a terminal event to be dreaded but part of a continuum of spiritual renewal that leads us back to home.

On this latter point, Paul is echoing the words of Jesus himself (in John 14:3-4) when he reassures his disciples by saying: "In my Father's house are many rooms...I am going there to prepare a place for you. And if I go and prepare a place for you, I will come back and take you to be with me that you also may be where I am."

Jesus will take in as many people as put their faith in him because, to borrow the words of Robert Frost: "Home is the place where, when you have to go there, they have to take you in."[19]

In my seminars, I often tell the story of a 70-year-old man who attended church services all his adult life without realising the necessity of inviting Christ into his life until it was almost too late. Coming under the conviction of the Holy Spirit one Easter Sunday, he turned to his pastor and asked:

"Will Jesus not be offended that I left it too late to come to him?"

"No not at all", replied his pastor. "Jesus has been waiting for you – to welcome you home!"

In turn, this story brings to mind the poem "The Hound of Heaven" by the English poet Francis Thompson; the central point of which concerns the ineluctable love of God, that would not let him go: The poem (all 182 stanzas of it!) opens with the confession: "I fled Him down the nights and down the days". But despite the poet's desperate efforts to hide and run away from God, he ended with total surrender: "I am he whom Thou you seekest."[20]

But while these stories help to illustrate that it is never too late to experience God's grace, it is important that we take a closer look at the Biblical concept of home-coming. More specifically, we have already noted in Paul's writings, that for those who put their faith in Christ, coming home (whether through acute sickness or the slow process of ageing) is not a one-time event but, rather, a *continuous*, daily, process of inward renewal.

Hence, it is no use worrying about whether one is 'ready to die' or not. What is required of us is something much simpler, namely the humble acknowledgement that whilst we are still alive, we are *already* dying and that *God's presence is our greatest need, at each and every moment of our lives.*

Of course, there is so much that we would like to know about life after death; and so many things we can't get our heads round. And, as we get older, it is natural (even for committed Christians) to be afraid of the pain that often comes with the process of dying. However, faith in Christ teaches us that when we are gradually stripped of everything that props us up (independence, health, dignity), we are left with more and more of God as we learn to dig into God's word. As we face the challenges that lie ahead, let us not doubt in the dark what God has revealed to us in the light of Christ.

"My presence will go with you, and I will give you rest." (Exodus 33:14)

"Though you have not seen him, you love him; even though you do not see him now, you believe in him, and are filled with inexpressible and glorious joy, for you are receiving the goal of your faith, the salvation of your souls." (1 Peter 1:8-9)

The truth and power of these words was brought home to me recently by two events. Among a pile of correspondence awaiting my return from a trip to the United States, was a letter from a dear friend whose wife for the past four years, had been receiving treatment for cancer. She was due to embark on another 18-week course of chemotherapy. But the latest CT scan had shown that the cancer was so widespread that further treatment had been ruled out. My friend wrote: "The focus now is on palliative care including a colostomy operation. A critical stage has been reached and the assurance of your prayers is a great comfort. She is remarkably peaceful and two words 'courage' and 'trust', anchored in God's love, are foremost in her mind and attitude".

The second event was the visit that my wife and I made to the Tate Modern Art Gallery in London. Having seen different works of art on display we decided to experience the Polish artist, Miroslaw Balka's exhibition entitled HOW IS IT. It takes the form of a huge wooden container and was introduced thus:

"'How shall I move forward?' you may ask yourself, as you stand at the threshold, confronted by the darkness ahead… Staring ahead into the black void of 'How Is It' simultaneously embodies the unknown and the familiar – the shipping container, luring you inwards through its recognisable form. 'How Is It' is only complete when you, the viewer, enters".

We accepted the invitation and joined the throng, some going in and others coming out. The container "focuses us inwards, both physically and psychologically" as we skirt along its walls creating our own journey as we navigate the void, occasionally bumping into others. As we made our way gingerly forward into the huge belly of the container, my wife held my hand tightly, with both of us finding solace in each other's company. And when we turned around to make our way out of the container, two things moved me deeply:

First, in the darkness we could see vaguely those coming in, although we knew they couldn't see us, an experience that brought to mind a quotation from a friend, who once told me that "you must be a sufferer to recognise it in other's eyes". We could see anxiety and apprehension on the faces of some of them because we had gone through what they were now going through.

Secondly, as we got closer to the main entrance on our way out, we again began to experience an undulating sensation caused by a mirage that made us feel as if there were steps on the wooden floor. This reminded me that in our earthly journey there is never a moment when we are completely "out of the woods' because as Paul reminds his Christian readers: "Now we see but a poor reflection as in a mirror, then we shall see face to face" (1 Corinthians13:12).

In conclusion, if we are here today and could be gone tomorrow (Psalm 90:10), is human life really of any value? A committed Christian's answer is an emphatic 'yes'. We are of great value to God and we are equipped in the crucified and risen Christ to show love to others, leaving a legacy of changed lives.

So, how then, should we approach our death? For Charles Spurgeon the answer was very clear. We should "live here like strangers and make the world not a house, but an inn, in which we sup and lodge, expecting to be on our journey home".[21] It is an approach to both life and death that was admirably exemplified in March 1981 when the preacher and Bible commentator Dr Martyn Lloyd Jones lay on his deathbed. From 1939 to 1968 he had served as a pastor of London's Westminster Chapel. Now, at the end of his life, he had lost the ability to speak. Indicating that he did not want any more prayers for his recovery, he wrote on a piece of paper: "Do not hold me back from glory."

If we know and love our Lord Jesus Christ, we ought to be looking forward to being with him, at the appointed time. Not a minute early, but dead on time!

CHAPTER 2

RETIREMENT IS A NEW ADVENTURE

"Experience is a comb life gives you after you lose your hair." (Judith Stern)[1]

The secret of worldly happiness has been defined as having something to do, someone to love, and something to look forward to. This definition applies to old and young alike. But it is really in older age that the full impact of this definition is felt.

However, the definition of "old age" and of attitudes thereto, can vary greatly depending on the cultural and religious traditions of an individual or their community. In the US, a popular bumper sticker declares that "growing older is mandatory, growing up is optional". The sentiment (and the humour it embodies) might get lost in translation when transported to other cultures. For example, in many countries (including my own country of Nigeria), the elderly enjoy high levels of social status and many people deliberately dress and style their hair in ways that accentuate rather than disguise their age.

Likewise, attitudes towards retirement are also

culturally and historically situated. For example, my over-active, 51 year old, London-based, son was surprised to hear me remind him that God told the Levites that they should "retire from their regular duty at the age of fifty'" and although they should "assist their brothers in performing their duties…they themselves must not do the work" (Numbers 8:25-26).

Indeed, for my son, and for many of his workaholic peers, the prospect of "not working" is not something to look forward to but something to dread. It's hard enough for them to turn their smartphones off on the weekend let alone to remind themselves of the injunction contained in Hebrews 4 to enjoy the "sabbath rest" and to remember that "anyone who enters God's rest also rests from their works, just as God did from his" (Hebrews 4:9-10).

Accordingly, in this chapter I will be concentrating on the importance of having "something to do" in retirement but not in the sense of full time paid employment. On the contrary, as we approach retirement it is essential that work becomes our servant and not our master; and that we refocus our energies on "being" (active and productive) instead of "doing" (a job).

Needless to say, this shift in perspective is easier said than done. For decades now, the ageing process has been given a very bad press; few people look forward happily to retirement; and many are scared of retirement or of even getting older. As the novelist Susan Ertz succinctly describes it: "Millions long for immortality who don't know what to do with themselves on a rainy Sunday afternoon".[2]

Not everybody, of course, is miserable about getting older. There is a good deal of wry humour contained in the simple, homespun, injunction that we should not regret growing old because "it is a privilege denied to many", a mordant echo of which can be found in Maurice Chevalier's observation that "old age isn't so bad when you consider the alternative".[3] Personally, however, I prefer the gentler reflections of the 19th century American philosopher, William James when he notes: "How pleasant is the day when we give up striving to be young or slender".[4]

Nevertheless, the truth is that retirement *does* take some getting used to; and the important thing is not to allow old age to define who we are and what we are capable of becoming. History is full of individuals who make their best contributions in old age. The Bible contains a good record of the elderly who lived out God's script for happiness in their old age, including: Abraham, Sarah, Jethro and Naomi in the Old Testament; and Simeon, Anna, and John the Elder in the New Testament. Their lives, and the lives of more contemporary "role model" retirees, are a useful reminder that, while the strength and beauty of youth is physical and temporal, the strength and beauty of old age is spiritual and eternal.

It is also helpful to draw upon the words of Paul in his letter to the Corinthians when he observes that the weaknesses of old age can be a source of strength and a gateway through which we experience the grace of our Lord.

"The Lord said to me, 'my grace is sufficient for you, for my power is made perfect in weakness'. Therefore, I will boast all the more gladly about my weakness, so that Christ's power may be made perfect in me. For when I am weak, then I am strong." (2 Corinthians 12:8-10)

Paul's words came back to me a few years ago as I was reflecting on a conversation I had just had with a genuine "golden oldie" at a supermarket checkout queue. I was watching an elderly woman in front of me, arranging her purchases spread out on the conveyor belt as she awaited her turn to pay. Out of the corner of my eye I watched as she double checked that there was enough money in her purse for the total bill. I knew the feeling; no one wants to be found a few pence short!

"Groceries seem to get heavier by the day don't they", I said.

"Yes", she said. "That's why I have to shop more often now".

Turning to look at me for the first time, she asked, with a twinkle in her eye, "How old do you think I am"?

"Oh No!", I thought, as my mind whizzed around an embarrassing memory. It had happened a few years before, while I was staying at a Christian Guest House in Jos, Nigeria. A visiting African American University Professor was also a guest there on a visit. We were the only guests having lunch that day and our conversation was going well until she asked me to guess her age. I made a quick calculation of what I thought was possibly her real age and then reduced it by ten years.

"You must be around...err, sixty-two"?

Laughing loudly, she dropped the bombshell.

"I am 55."

She had rather enjoyed my embarrassment but then went on to explain that she had become completely grey by the time she finished her first degree.

Fortunately, the lady at the supermarket didn't have time to wait until I could figure out a winning answer as she proudly announced: "I am 83. How about you"?

"78" I replied.

Looking me over, she said, "You look good".

"And you too", I honestly responded.

On my way home I wondered what had become of the time-honoured woman's right to keep her age secret. It brought to mind a scene in Meike Ziervogel's novella, 'Clara's Daughter', in which the elderly Clara looks at herself in the mirror and comes to terms with her ageing body with the following reflections: "I have not looked in a mirror while naked for a long time. Wrinkly, baggy skin is not a pretty sight. But now as I am looking at myself I am oddly surprised. Yes, my breast and my tummy are hanging, my skin looks baggy. I am an old woman after all. But it is not ugly. This is skin that tells of experience and life."[5]

"Yes!", I said to myself as my mind reverted to another of Paul's instructions to the Corinthians where he enjoined them (two thousand years before

Meike Ziervogel) not to lose heart. "Though outwardly we are wasting away, yet inwardly we are being renewed day by day" (2 Corinthians 4:16).

In other words, a "graceful" retirement is one that entails a wholesome recognition of human frailty and mortality and of the strength and power of our Lord. A graceful retirement also requires a humble acknowledgement that our physical weakness is part of an essential process by which we gradually pass on the baton to the next generation.

For a good biblical illustration of this process of intergenerational transfer, we can draw upon the example of Jethro who ploughed back his management skills into Moses, his son-in-law. Among other things, he warned Moses against the dangers of micro-management and stressed the need to delegate.

"You and these people who come to you will only wear yourselves out. The work is too heavy for you; you cannot handle it alone. Listen now to me and I will give you some advice, and may God be with you. Select capable men from all the people – men who fear God, trustworthy men who hate dishonest gain – and appoint them as officials over thousands, hundreds, fifties and tens. Have them serve as judges for the people at all times, but have them bring every difficult case to you; the simple cases they can decide themselves. That will make your load lighter, because they will share it with you. If you do this and God so commands, you will be able to stand the strain, and all these people will go home satisfied." (Exodus 18:18-23)

As the saying goes, a new broom sweep clean, but an old broom knows the corners! Wisely, Moses respected the management advice of his non-Jewish father-in-law and did exactly what he said. In turn, Jethro's relationship with his son-in-law appears to have triggered a conversion experience as instanced by Jethro's declaration that: "Now I know that the Lord is greater than all the other gods for he did this to those who had treated Israel arrogantly" (Exodus 18:11). This relationship between Jethro and Moses serves as a good example not just of nurturing (and reciprocal) generational interchange but also as a model for healthy cross-cultural marital alliances.

In the foregoing, I have attempted, albeit rather circuitously, to illustrate my belief that a graceful retirement is a life of continuing usefulness. As for *how* to achieve this goal, my own experience (derived as much from my mistakes as from any successes) has taught me that there are five essential pieces of mental and spiritual equipment that can help us along the way. As listed below, they are:

i. A new identity – derived from coming to terms with the real you.
ii. A new set of priorities – reflected in better time management.
iii. A new perspective – acquired by learning to see things through God's eyes.
iv. A new humility – wherein we learn the value of contentment.
v. A new confidence – which accepts that testing goes hand in hand with trusting.

In the sections that follow, I will briefly elaborate

on each of these spiritual accoutrements.

1. A new identity – derived from coming to terms with the real you

"The closing years of life are like a masquerade party, when masks are dropped." (Schopenhauer)[6]

As we enter into retirement, we need to recover the joy of 'being' instead of the relentless preoccupation with 'doing'. This is because our true identities derive more from who we are in our relationships than from what we do.

Dr. William H. Thomas, a geriatric specialist, has rightly pointed out that babies begin life by being. As we approach adulthood, the emphasis shifts to accomplishment. Then as we grow older and our energy wanes, we must refocus on being. Elder-hood brings us full circle to a life that favours being over doing. This is a gift of great value.[7]

It takes humility and acceptance to enjoy the limitation that ageing brings. As the bible says in John 21:18-19: "I tell you the truth, when you were younger you dressed yourself and went where you wanted; but when you are old you will stretch out your hands, and someone will dress you and lead where you do not want to go".

This is the eventual reality of the ageing process and there is no use denying it. Or, as the poet Philip Larkin puts it, old age – for far too many people – is experienced as a "hideous inverted childhood".[8]

The great thing about mature age is that it gives us

the opportunity to carve out an identity that is less dependent on what we do than on who we are. Or to borrow a piece of contemporary jargon, it allows us to engage in – and become proficient at – the practice of 'mindfulness' wherein we allow our bodies and souls to just 'be' in the moment, to observe and feel and connect with others without rushing to judgement or trying to fit our thoughts into a plan of 'action'.

As I will attempt to explain below, it is also critically important that we recognize that 'mindfulness' can be co-existent with a loss of our cognitive capacities or those of our loved ones. If we hone our capacities for 'being' rather than doing we will strengthen our abilities to commune and connect with other human 'beings' even when we (or they) have lost our capacity for certain physical or cognitive actions.

I was reminded, recently, that the word 'patient' derives from the Latin word *'pati'* meaning 'to suffer'. It describes one who suffers patiently. In its brochure, the Alzheimer's Society (the UK's largest dementia charity) describes Alzheimer's as "a thief that robs you of everything you value". It is estimated that one in three over-65 people in UK suffers from this degenerative disease; and the number of people in the UK who have a relative or friend living with dementia is estimated at nearly 25 million. As for what it is actually like to be in the presence of an Alzheimer's sufferer, the truth is that everyone's experience is different. But, by way of illustration, I will recount one of my own experiences.

In January 2011, I had been spending a lot of time thinking about my Christian friends who were suffering from Alzheimer's or other forms of dementia. That week, I accompanied a retired missionary to visit a former colleague who is now in a nursing home. She had served as a missionary for three decades in Africa. She was a prolific Christian writer on cross-cultural issues and on relationships between missionaries and emerging indigenous African leaders. She was, for many years, my stimulating sparring partner on issues relating to reciprocal partnership in world mission. She retired early from her missionary service to look after her father who was suffering from Alzheimer's. She wrote a book afterwards describing graphically her experience of looking after him.

Just a few years later she, a single lady, also became a victim of Alzheimer's and with no family member to look after her, agreed to move into a nursing home.

I went with her closest missionary friend to see her there. We waited for half an hour in the nursing home's waiting lounge to give her time to finish her lunch. Eventually my companion went to fetch her. Although I didn't know what to expect, nothing in my imagination had prepared me for the sight of the much-diminished shell of my dear friend as I was about to kiss her. Looking about half her normal weight, she immediately wondered if we had met before. She kept murmuring something to herself. And as she sat next to me I noticed that she was wearing odd socks on her feet. She kept fidgeting and looking around vacantly as if she was looking for something. She wanted to go for a walk outside even though it was raining. I tried in vain to jog her memory about some of the things we used to discuss and I thought there was a flicker of comprehension when she said "I have done all that" before changing the subject to "Do you live here?" and pointing to the table in the centre of the lounge and asking, "What is that for?".

My co-visitor off-loaded to her the content of a bag of goodies she had brought for her – an assortment of biscuits and chocolates of different sizes and colours – to last until her next visit. She immediately prised open one chocolate packet and quickly unwrapped one, ate it, and pulled out another and noticing the ridge in the middle, broke it, put one half in her mouth and gave me the other half as a small girl would do knowing that that there were still more left in the box. After a short while my fellow visitor took the sweets to her bedroom, after which we prayed before we said our goodbye.

Looking back on that visit a quotation from Michael Banner came to mind:

"People with Alzheimer's can seem to fade away before our very eyes. The world has always had invisible people – in Jesus' day they were widows, lepers, the poor and the outcast. And in the stories told about Jesus, he seems to have an uncanny eye for those who might otherwise be overlooked and excluded from community. When people talk of the 'death of the person', such ways of speaking are not to be discounted – they plainly express a profound sense of losing someone as they succumb to dementia. But this manner of speaking ought not to be accepted without

question. Apart from everything else, the imagery is in danger of discouraging us from caring for the demented before we have even started, since if we take it literally, there is no one there to care for. But as our cognitive capacities fail, the people we once were may still be there, perhaps in fragments. I may forget who I am, or who you are, but finding and sustaining what remains of the person in their diminished state is surely the task and the challenge, which confronts us."9

My friend's confusion and incomprehension did upset me; but I felt better for visiting her; and I knew then that I needed further reflection on my reaction. For even when we begin to notice memory slips in ourselves, or in the life of a loved one, God's word is still there, "stored up" "or "treasured" in the heart (Psalm 119:11). Nothing, not even our failing memories "can separate us from the love of God in Christ Jesus" (Romans 8:39).

Learning to "be" will surely help us come to terms with our own cognitive failings and with the failings of others; and it will help us to appreciate others' physical and spiritual presence (their eyes, smile, their touch, their voice) irrespective of whether they even "recognise" us (or vice-versa!). But will these exercises in the joy of "being" help us to deal with the increasingly fraught problems presented by modern medical science and its ability to prolong our lives beyond the temporal boundaries of earlier eras? For example, if we accept the words of David Winter that "the gift of God is not simply duration but the quality of life", what should we make of the contemporary debate over the ethics of assisted suicide?

In their book, entitled "Easeful Death", Mary Warnock and Elizabeth Macdonald present a cogent case for the legalisation of assisted suicide. The main thrust of their argument is the distinction they make between the "biological" and "autobiographical" life of a unique individual who possesses his/her own experiences. More specifically, they question whether, once the autobiographical life is over, continued life is always in the best interests of a person "irredeemably suffering" from Alzheimer's or other forms of dementia. In their view, we should be prepared "to contemplate not merely allowing him to die by withholding treatment if he falls ill, but actually and compassionately causing his death."[10]

By contrast, in his book entitled "A Time to Live", my good friend, Revd. George Pitcher, mounts an equally compelling case against euthanasia and assisted suicide. The central thrust of his argument is that "we should concentrate all our human effort on the relief of suffering, an effort that is undermined once death has become a clinical option". For, as he sees it, "once the disabled are enabled to dispose of themselves, they become disposable".[11]

"Life is given to no one as a freehold; we all hold it on leasehold." (Lucretius)[12]

As an octogenarian, I feel fortunate in the knowledge that I am probably too old for any new 21st century medical innovations to extend my tenancy on life beyond the point where it is sufferable (either by me or my loved ones). But that luxury may not be extended to my children or grandchildren and I fear they will be faced with ethical dilemmas the like of which I cannot even begin to contemplate. Nevertheless, even when it comes to their turn to enter into old age and senescence, my belief is that neither a pre-emptive action (assisted suicide) nor a belief in life after death will see any of us go "unduly troubled" through "the valley of the shadow of death". Instead, it is learning to embrace and cooperate with (rather than resent and resist) the inevitable that may help us to be better prepared for all eventualities.

2. A new set of priorities – reflected in better time management

Retirement brings home the fact that time doesn't fly; we do! Time stays the same; maintaining sixty seconds per minute, and twenty-four hours per day. It takes retirement for most people to realise how brief the human life span is. "He who will lead a good life", declares Bishop Ryle "must always think of his last days"; an injunction that echoes the words of Psalm 39:4-5: "Show me, O Lord, my life's end and the number of my days; let me know how fleeting my life is. You have made my days a mere handbreadth; the span of life is as nothing before you. Each man's life is like a breath".

There is nothing morbid about the Psalmist's prayer. Nor do these verses imply that we should count each second. They are simply a reminder that, when we consider the fleeting nature of life, we should be mindful of the importance of using our time wisely.

King David's description of life, as "a mere handbreadth" is a powerful metaphor which challenges us to put our house in order, and not leave others to clear up the mess we may leave behind. For example, whilst we all know that making a legally binding will is of critical importance to our loved ones, studies conducted in 2017 showed that 60% of adults in the UK had not made a will. Those aged 55 and over were more likely to have a will than those aged 18-34. However, even in the older age group, more than a third (37%) of adults were still without one. In other words, millions of people needlessly run the risk of dying intestate and having their estate distributed solely according to intestacy law, which may not reflect their wishes.

Mindful of this fact, shortly after my retirement, my wife and I updated our will and power of attorney well in advance of becoming incapacitated. In the years since, I have become more conscious than ever that we are here today, and could be gone tomorrow. It is said that the best among us is remembered for perhaps a hundred years or so. The rest of us are soon forgotten. The memory of past generations and inscriptions on our graves soon fade away. Yet our legacy can be passed on through our family and through the impact we have made on people's lives.

"Naked a man comes from his mother's womb, and as he comes, so he departs. He takes nothing from his labour that he can carry in his hand." (Ecclesiastes 5:15-16)

Ironically, it is the unwillingness to face the fact that we will all eventually die that prevents many from putting pen to legal paper in making a will. Indeed, for many people, the act of making a will feels akin to signing a death warrant. In reality, however, it is one of the most life-affirming things that we can do because it focuses our energies not on death but on the lives of people that we know and love.

For some of us, it may also be important to remember that in certain communities, women – whether by law or by custom and practice – are not permitted to inherit property (or can only inherit certain types of assets). Thus, wherever possible, it is essential that we strive to ensure that the rights of beneficiaries of our inheritance are legally protected, valid, binding and enforceable.

Moreover, physical assets need not be the only things that we formally hand over to our inheritors. We can, for example, draw up an additional, non-binding, "ethical" (or "autobiographical") statement which can be used to pass down ethical values from one generation to another. This document is typically a statement of the beliefs and guiding principles that we entrust to future generations in the hope that they will adhere to the same. It can comprise a single powerful sentence or life motto e.g. "For me to live is Christ, to die is gain" (Philippians 1:21) or it can be a much longer treatise.

Deuteronomy 4:9 provides an eloquent theological precedent for making an ethical/autobiographical will: "Only be careful, and watch yourselves closely so that you do not forget the things your eyes have seen or let them slip from your heart as long as you live. Teach them to your children and to their children after them."

Indeed, an essential part of Christian stewardship entails being good custodians of our life story. God commanded the Israelites, as they approached the Promised Land; to ensure that their children and grandchildren knew their family history, and were told of how God had worked things out for them, sometimes in humanly impossible situations. Each of us has a unique story to tell of how God's steadfastness has strengthened our faith and helped us overcome our doubts and disappointments.

In short, to leave a lasting legacy for our children, we should depend on the Lord (Genesis 4:1) and pray for them (Job 1:5). But it is essential that we don't forget to write our wills! Both of them: the legal will and the ethical/autobiographical will.

Having first ensured that our testamentary affairs are in good order, prudential retirement behaviour may also require that we exercise care and foresight in the more commonplace areas of our life. For example, I am unlikely to forget the moment, at 4am on Thursday 5 January 2006, that I was reminded of the reason for installing a handrail on the staircase in our new home. I was fast asleep when I heard (or thought I heard) a loud bang as if someone was trying to break into our house. I crept out of the bedroom quietly so as not to awaken my wife, and proceeded to go downstairs to investigate. Then an earth-shaking crash brought my wife to the top of the staircase (and no doubt made the family next door wonder what we were doing to each other!).

It was my eleven-stone bodyweight cascading down the stairs that caused the noise. As I sat there, stunned and shaken, the verse of the Bible I had meditated on the day before came back to comfort me: "He who dwells in the shadow of the Most High will rest in the shadow of the Almighty" (Psalm 91:1).

I felt incredibly calm, which, come to think of it, must have frightened my wife before she switched on the light. Although I was knocked about a bit, the good Lord must have "commanded his angels…to guard me" (Psalm 91:11). Thankfully, all I had to show for my fall were a bruised left calf, a small tear on my elbow, a small cut on my left ankle and a five-pence sized bump on my forehead. My wife dusted me down, dressed up my self-inflicted wounds, made me a cup of tea and ordered me to bed.

I never did find out the source of the original noise that woke me up in the first place. But I learned the hard way that the handrail is not there for decoration but for support and safety and that, for people of my age, moving around the house in the dark can be extremely dangerous. I am unlikely to forget that experience because my ageing body cannot cope with another fall.

Ever since, I have become extra careful in using the handrail on the staircase or escalators because I don't intend to abuse the grace of God by putting my safety at risk.

"Death is a long journey and you can't take anything to read on it" (Drue Heinz).[13]

Other essential elements in the art of good retirement "housekeeping" include downsizing and decluttering exercises. In my own case, shortly after my retirement, I started to downsize all my belongings, beginning with my filling cabinets. I also made a determined effort to travel light and to rid myself of clutter, including unused or unloved clothing items. Subsequently, the occasional appearance of moths has provided me with additional incentives to thin out my wardrobe and I have now made several visits to our local charity shop. Indeed, when my daughter teases me that I have become a devotee of Marie Kondo (the television celebrity who teaches people how to de-clutter their homes) I am more than happy to plead guilty as charged.

"Ok, so once you've drawn up your last will and testament and got your physical home in ship-shape condition and you've downsized and decluttered…what next?! What do you do with all the time that you've freed up?" This, more or less, was the question that I found myself asking at the beginning of my retirement. By way of response, I set myself three simple objectives: a) to acquire basic computer skills so as to be able to send and receive email; b) to be able do what my daughter describes as "rudimentary cooking"; and c) to make use of opportunities to plough back the ministry experience I had gained over the years.

However, although these objectives seemed

simple at the time, in practice their continuing attainment has proved more challenging – and rewarding – than I could have imagined. In the process, I have also learned that one's post-retirement objectives should not be set in stone because retirement demands a willingness to flex and adapt to changing circumstances. Operating systems and email software change at an ever bewildering pace; my oven now has a bigger (electronic) memory than I do; and the meetings in which I can minister to people increasingly take place 'virtually' via Zoom calls or Facetime.

Nevertheless, nearly twenty years on, not only am I still striving to meet my original objectives but the accumulated years of 'trying' have enriched my life and given me the confidence to cope with the challenges of getting older. It's great to be able to entertain my family and friends; to keep in touch by email, text and Zoom calls; and to have occasional 'real life' opportunities to plough back my ministry experience. In turn, each of these activities has helped me to endeavour to keep in step with the Holy Spirit and to keep abreast of what God is doing around the world. Thus, as each year goes by, I cherish more and more the verses contained in Ephesians 5:15-20 which are reproduced below:

"Look carefully then how you walk, not as unwise but as wise, making the best use of the time, because the days are evil. Therefore do not be foolish, but understand what the will of the Lord is. And do not get drunk with wine, for that is debauchery, but be filled with the Spirit, addressing one another

in psalms and hymns and spiritual songs, singing and making melody to the Lord with your heart, giving thanks always and for everything to God the Father in the name of our Lord Jesus Christ."

3. A new perspective – acquired by learning to see things through God's eyes

"You can't depend on your eyes when your imagination is out of focus." (Mark Twain)[14]

If we focus our attention on God in prayer, though our circumstances may not change immediately, our perspective can. As the psalmist puts it: "My flesh and my heart may fail, but God is the strength of my heart and my portion forever" (Psalm 73:26). John Wesley's younger brother once said to him, "If God gives me wings, I will fly". John replied by saying, "If God bid me fly, I will trust him for the wings".

Retirement for many in the developed world (especially those with index-linked pensions) is a time to relax, travel, or engage in hobbies. Nevertheless, for many of these lucky individuals, it is all too easy to lose perspective and fail to remember that such a comfortable lifestyle is beyond the reach of even the 'educated' professional senior citizens of the developing world, where out of necessity, many elderly people work themselves to death. Indeed, I frequently encounter high levels of anxiety and dissatisfaction amongst people who have forgotten how to count their blessings.

I lay the blame for some of this amnesia on the

relentless pace of modern secular life and the diminished opportunities for people to engage in activities of quiet contemplation. The situation is aptly summed up by Archbishop Rowan Williams when he notes that: "Increasingly, one of the marks of a fully and uncompromisingly secular environment is the notion of undifferentiated time. There are, for mature late capitalism no such things as the weekends. The problem with this kind of secularism is not so much a denial of the existence of God as the denial of the possibility of leisure – of time that is not spent in serving the market".[15]

Not surprisingly, after a long working career where time is insufficiently differentiated and there's "never enough time", the transition to retirement can come as a disorienting shock to many people. They now have plenty of contemplative time in which to count their blessings but little, if any, prior practice in the same. Hence the effort to "put things in perspective" is often a good deal harder than it would otherwise have been.

This is why I am such a firm believer in the importance of a good diet, regular physical exercise and sleep hygiene. In my experience, their value lies not just in the physical benefits that they bring, but in their capacity to help reset our mental perspectives and calm our anxieties. A gentle early morning or evening stroll can make a world of difference to one's physical and mental health. However, because of the unreliable British weather, I now go to the gym two or three times a week. At my age, what I don't use I may so easily lose. And I find the best anti-dote for overtired mood swings is a lunchtime nap!

But there is, of course, a limit to the perspective-shifting powers of one's physical exercises; and the older we get the more we need to rely upon spiritual exercises to help us put our infirmities and anxieties into proper perspective. This is especially true whenever we encounter experiences that we may be tempted to classify as 'worst case' scenarios.

As Bishop Tutu once remarked, these worst case scenarios "may give God a better chance to get our attention"[16]; a truth which came home to me in full-colour animation one afternoon a couple of years ago. From the top of a double-decker bus I could see a man with a bulging briefcase frantically running to catch the bus I was on as it approached the next bus stop. Just as he was about to hop on the bus, his briefcase involuntarily opened up, tipping all its contents onto the wet pavement. As the bus moved on, and the poor man was left behind trying to salvage his papers, the man sitting in front of me blurted out what was on the minds of many of us: "It doesn't get much worse than that!".

That left me wondering if the man was running late for an important assignment, an interview perhaps or an important office presentation. A worst-case scenario (such as the one we had just witnessed) is whatever leaves us feeling doomed, hopeless and despairing of a good outcome. It is whatever seems to us a once in a lifetime opportunity abruptly coming to nothing. It is whatever seems to us like a titanic or tsunami-like cascade of bad luck.

It can be something personally and painfully

experienced: financial loss, the death of a loved one or a confirmation of a terminal illness. It's what grieving parents, especially of young adults, go through. It is the sort of thing that made Mary say despairingly to Jesus "If you had been here my brother would not have died" (John 11:21). Likewise, for our Lord's first disciples, Good Friday was a worst possible scenario; and at that particular moment in time, the joy of Easter Sunday must have seemed a staggering impossibility.

But when it comes to depictions of the worst case scenario, the book of Job takes the biblical biscuit. Yet it was Job's relationship with God that gave him the inner strength to cope with his adversity. He said "God knows the way I take: when he has tested me, I shall come forth as gold" (Job 23:10).

So as the bus journey continued, there I was reflecting on the fact that we all live within the shadow of the worst-case scenario. However, four stops down the road, one impatient cyclist tried to jump the traffic light and was knocked down by our bus. Fortunately, he wasn't fatally injured. Nevertheless, we were all held up for some time while an ambulance was called and our driver was interviewed by the police and statements were taken from some fellow passengers. We then all disembarked to catch another bus while the traffic police continued with their investigation.

However, the traffic jam created by the accident meant that the buses behind us were all full by the time they reached our stranded location. Among the passengers in one of the buses that drove past us, I spotted the same man who had failed to catch our stricken bus. And, at least in my imagination, he seemed to be smiling! Indeed, it was a perfect reminder that what may appear to us as a 'worst case scenario' may be nothing more than an intimation of God's gracious intervention. In the words of Dame Julian of Norwich "there is no blame in God". [17] And, as Desmond Tutu has observed, it is only our failure to recognise this that makes us "spend so much time staring despairingly at the door that has just closed that we don't notice that hope has just opened a window".[18]

On the subsequent Good Friday, it struck me that for a Christian the 'shock absorber' against all manner of 'worst-case scenarios' is the following verse from Galatians 2:20: "I have been crucified with Christ, I no longer live, but Christ lives in me. The life I live in the body, I live by faith in the Son of God, who loved me and gave himself for me." It is also comforting for a committed Christian to know that "it is God who works in you to will and to act according to his good purpose" (Philippians 2:13).

"Success is moving from failure to failure without losing enthusiasm" (Anon.)[19]

When faced with a worst-case scenario we need to pray to be released from our grip on fear so that we can be emboldened to cling to God's loving kindness and his faithfulness. In Psalm 61:2, when David sings "Lead me to a rock that is higher than I", he is recognising the need to see things from God's perspective. This perspective is what sculptors call 'hyper-seeing'. It is the artist's ability to look at a rough piece of stone and see it in its final perfected form. It is a good description of how God works and a powerful reminder that, whenever we are tempted to despair, we should remember that God's omniscience extends far beyond our own myopic field of vision.

4. A new humility – wherein we learn the value of contentment.

"If, God forbid, I am struck gravely ill in my last days, I pray I won't have the effrontery to complain; after such a largesse having been poured on me for decades, that would be outrageously ungrateful." (Alec Guinness)[20]

In the quotation above, Alec Guinness might have been reflecting on the words of the Psalmist when he says: "Be at peace once more, O my soul, for the Lord has been good to you".

For Sir Alec, a famous and wealthy retiree, the spiritual danger to be avoided was that of ingratitude caused by a failure to reflect upon his good fortune relative to so many others. But for many people, especially those in economically unstable countries, the more pressing danger is not wealthy ingratitude but the stress, desperation and social shame occasioned by a searing descent into poverty.

In the developing parts of the world (including my own birthplace, Nigeria), uncontrollable macro-economic circumstances make it particularly difficult for middle-class retirees to come to terms with their greatly reduced pension income. Many of them are well educated, highly respected professionals who diligently saved as much as they could for their retirement and refused to engage in unscrupulous methods of providing for their 'rainy days', such as corruption, exploitation, or abuse of power. Yet, upon entering retirement, they encounter – all too often – the bitter reality that, despite their best efforts to live within their means, the value of their savings and pensions has been drastically eroded.

Firstly, the regular depreciation of the value of the national currency of many developing countries means that the real purchasing power of their pensions can fall precipitously in a very short space of time. And to make matters worse, these pensions are rarely paid on time (if at all). Secondly, the depreciating hard currency value of their retirement income means that when they become sick they often can't afford to maintain their health insurance or purchase prescribed medicine in time to prevent morbidity or mortality. And going aboard for treatment is no longer an option for many of these previously well-heeled retirees. Third, and most stressful of all, there are the insatiable demands of extended family members on their meagre income.

It is easy to say that the solution to post-retirement impoverishment in developing countries is better government; but institutional development is a slow process that occurs over several generations. Hence for retirees living today in these countries, their material situation is unlikely to change for the better within the relatively short lifespan that is left to them.

Cognisant of this fact, many of them realise, too late, the wisdom of the plea contained in Proverbs 30:7-9: "Two things I ask of you, O Lord; do not refuse me before I die: Give me neither poverty nor riches; but give me only my daily bread. Otherwise, I may have too much and disown you and say 'who is the Lord?' Or I may become poor and steal and dishonour the name of my God."

It is true that both prosperity and adversity can destroy our contentment. But it is prosperity *followed by* adversity that poses the greatest challenge to our faith and our capacity to be at peace with ourselves and with the world. Nevertheless, even when our circumstances have been drastically reduced (and there is no realistic prospect of our material conditions improving within our remaining lifespan), we can still find peace and contentment if we remember that God has already given us all we need.

"For we brought nothing into the world, and we can take nothing out of it. But if we have food and clothing, we will be content with that." (1 Timothy 6:7-8)

A Christian's contentment is not based on his circumstances, but on his relationship with Christ. Thus, true contentment will enable you to grow wherever God has planted you. It is a state of mind and spirit that has been valued by philosophers down the ages, from the stoic Epictetus to the glamorous Ingrid Bergman.

"Don't demand that things happen as you wish, but wish that they happen as they do happen, and you will go on well." (Epictetus)[21]

"Worry never robs tomorrow of its sorrow, it only saps today of its strength." (A J Cronin)[22]

"Success is getting what you want; happiness is wanting what you get." (Ingrid Bergman)[23]

An elderly African man watching a new missionary unload his belongings told him: "Let me know if you need anything, and I will show you how to do without it."

5. A new confidence – which accepts that testing goes hand in hand with trusting

As articulated in the previous section, the real test of where our confidence lies is how we react in the face of infirmity or adversity. All of us want things that we don't really need and it's never easy for us to consciously interrupt this mental process and tailor our desires to our material or physical circumstances. But perhaps one way we can ease this transition is by embracing the concept of "peaceful anxiety".

But is such a contradictory mental state really possible? That was my initial reaction to a remark made by a Christian guest speaker when he learned that he had been refused a visa to travel abroad. When asked how he was feeling by a colleague he replied: "I am experiencing peaceful anxiety". Seeing that his coworker looked confused, he quickly explained: "I have had anxiety because I need the visa. But right now, I have great peace because I know that, after all, there is nothing I can do about it."

As I travel ever further into the ninth decade of my life, I am learning afresh that the secret of peace is to hand over every anxious thought to God (Isaiah 26:3-4). I am also increasingly comforted by the example of the two women who feature most prominently in the account of the nativity, namely Elizabeth and her cousin Mary.

At first, both of these women experienced deep anxieties, tension and frustrations. Elizabeth despaired of having the baby she so desperately wanted, because she was well past the age of child bearing (Luke 1:37). For Mary, on the other hand, marriage not pregnancy was uppermost in her mind and, at first, she was "deeply troubled" by her encounter with the angel Gabriel and his apparent suggestion that she would have a child before the consummation of her marriage to Joseph, an event that would normally attract severe social stigma.

But Elizabeth and Mary also came to experience the peace that comes from submission to God's will. "The Lord has done this for me," said Elizabeth when she finally became pregnant and "he has shown his favor and taken away my disgrace among the people" (Luke 1:23). Likewise, Mary, after listening to the angel Gabriel, although she undoubtedly remained anxious, humbly declared: "I am the Lord's servant. May it be to me as you have said" (Luke 1:38).

The example of Elizabeth and Mary is a wonderful

reminder that, for a committed Christian, testing cannot be separated from trusting. It is also a poignant illustration that no matter how old we are or how barren our life circumstances, we can still assist in the joyous hand-over of life to the next generation.

I know that going through "the valley of the shadow of death" is likely to be the ultimate human adventure. And that few of us will come to the end of our journey without some pain. But it is a great comfort to have the companionship of the Lord Jesus Christ who knows the way through the uncharted waters of our final journey (John 14:1-2).

When our children were old enough to go to college, work or parties on their own, I always stayed awake until they returned home. "How did it go?" or "How did you get on?", I would ask. They would usually reply by saying: "Fine" or "Pretty good". But when they had gone through a difficult time, they would say: "It is good to be home". So it is comforting to know that at the end of our earthly journey, our heavenly Father will be there waiting for our arrival and we too will be saying to him: "It is sure good to be home" (Philippians 3:20-21).

"Old age can be a pathway home. Shall we not feel tired at the end of the mountain climb? But we are nearly home! Does that not make up for it?" (Rhena Taylor).[24]

CHAPTER 3

DEEPENING OF LOVING RELATIONSHIPS

"Age does not protect you from love. But love, to some extent, protects you from age." (Jeanne Moreau)[1]

Old age is a time when we lose not only our relatives but also our closest friends, whether through relocation, terminal illness or death. It is a time when we begin to see our relationship with God, families, and close friends in new light, because for many of us they are all we have left.

A Portuguese proverb says: "In the end you only have five true friends and the rest is landscape" and the older we get the closer we come to a true understanding of Voltaire's dictum that "where there is friendship there is our homeland".[2]

As the number of Christmas and birthday cards decreases, we must learn to deepen our relationship with God and with our families and friends. How to do this is the aim of this third chapter. This is because in retirement, more than at any other time, close and loving relationships are a necessary condition for our well-being (physical, psychological and spiritual).

The scriptures provide us with several examples of the blessings that derive from such relationships. And, of these, my favourite is the story of Naomi and Ruth. When we first encounter Naomi, we learn that her husband and her two sons have died. She is adrift in a foreign land and is living in an impecunious state with her two daughters-in-law. She decides to pack her things and head home to her ancestral town of Bethlehem in Judah. Before she departs, she says goodbye to her two daughters-in-law and says to them:

"Go back, each of you, to your mother's home. May the Lord show you kindness, as you have shown kindness to your dead husbands and to me. May the Lord grant that each of you will find rest in the home of another husband." (Ruth 1:8)

Naomi's name in Hebrew means "the pleasant one" and she certainly lived up to this name. She insists that both her daughters-in-law (Orpah and Ruth) must act in their own best interest and she seeks to free them of any filial obligations. This selflessness is a role model for all people of riper age.

However, Naomi quickly learns the truth of the saying that we make our friends, but God gives us our in-laws. Ruth rejects her entreaties to leave and insists on travelling with Naomi into Judah. Her words have echoed down the generations ever since:

Don't urge me to leave you or to turn back from you. Where you go I will go, and where you stay I will stay. Your people will be my people and your God my God. (Ruth:1:16)

The loving relationship between Naomi and Ruth is further illustrated when the two women arrive in Bethlehem, penniless and vulnerable. Ruth goes out every day to work as a field hand; but her situation is transformed when she catches the eye of a man called Boaz who is not only a strong "man of standing" but a person of great kindness and gentleness. Upon hearing of this, Naomi uses the wisdom of age to counsel her daughter-in-law on her next steps. Amongst other things, she advises her to:

"Wash, put on perfume, and get dressed in your best clothes. Then go down to the threshing floor, but don't let him know you are there until he has finished eating and drinking." (Ruth 3:3)

To cut a long story short, thanks to Naomi's sage advice, Ruth gets her guy and eventually gives birth to Obed who became the grandfather of David in the genealogy of the Saviour of the world.

The experiences of Naomi and Ruth can serve as a signboard to the five key relationships that we need to nurture in our retirement years, namely those with:

i. Our God;
ii. Our adversaries (both living and deceased);
iii. Ourselves (including our personal demons);
iv. Our family and close friends; and
v. Our local church.

1. Deepening our relationship with God

"The older I get the less I believe and the more I believe more deeply." (anon)

Retirement helps us to see how frantic engagement in activities (whether Christian or secular) can subconsciously obscure the reality of our true self and make it difficult to experience what it really means to heed the Lord when he tells us to "be still and know that I am God". (Psalm 46:10).

Having a regular quiet time with the Lord is essential for continuing spiritual growth in Christ. It is akin to what oceanographers call a "slack tide" i.e. the period when the tide is neither too high nor too low and the water is described as "unstressed". This slack tide is a quiet pause before the surging of the tidal flow begins again. Correspondingly, a daily commune with God will help to "quiet you with his love" (Zephaniah 3:17).

As we deepen our relationship with God, the two daily spiritual practices that become especially important in old age are those of patience and thankfulness.

Patience is a virtue that can be all too easily lost in the melee of modern life where our senses are attuned to 'instant messages', 'one-click ordering' and 'same day' Amazon deliveries. This relentless and impatient world is very different from the world of my youth where patience was understood not just as a gift but as a habit of mind cultivated through daily practice.

By way of illustration, I often recount the story of

a conference speaker who was delayed for a couple of hours because of car trouble. A newly arrived missionary was surprised that hardly any of the welcoming congregation left and that the guest speaker was given an enthusiastic reception on his arrival. Sensing the missionary's bafflement, the local pastor explained: "We know the longer we wait the sooner he will come; we will easily forget how long we've waited when God's servant delivers God's message to us. It will be worth the waiting!"

This coupling of patience and praise finds echoes in the words of the Psalmist when he recalls how he "waited patiently for the Lord"; how the Lord heard his cry; lifted him "out of the mud and mire"; gave him a "firm place to stand"; and put a new song in his mouth, "a hymn of praise to our God" (Psalm 40:1-3).

In my active years as a pastor, I was often conscious of my disinclination to engage in overt displays of praise-giving. Now that I am in retirement, I have more time to reflect on the true meaning and value of the concept of praise and I have derived great comfort and insight from the Old-Testament books of Job, Deuteronomy, Chronicles, Nehemiah, Esther and Ruth. For example, I often find myself returning to the words spoken by Moses in Deuteronomy 10:21, viz. "He is your praise; he is your God who performed wonders you saw with your own eyes".

The Scottish minister Alexander Whyte knew God to be his praise because he always found something to praise God for even in the bleakest of situation. On a dark Sunday morning when the weather was freezing wet and stormy, one of his deacons whispered "I am sure the pastor will have nothing to thank God for today". On cue, their pastor began by praying: "We thank God that the weather is not always like this".

The lives of Moses and Alexander Whyte were separated by several millennia. But each of them remind us that, if God is our praise, we will never be short of what we can thank him for every moment of the day, because a heart at peace with God will always have reasons to praise him. Whyte's dry turn of phrase also reminds us that praising God is not a solicitous activity. For, as Marilynne Robinson has noted, "God does not need our worship. We worship him to enlarge our sense of the holy, so that we may feel and know the presence of the Lord, who is with us always".[3] It is the conscious awareness of God in our lives that pleases him and Christians will be a lot happier in this life if they think less about what they can do to please God and more on the closeness of his presence in their lives.

C S Lewis in his early Christian life also baulked at the idea of heaping praise upon a God for the misguided sake of trying to please him. As he pithily remarked, the whole world "rings with praise" and the last thing God needs is any attempt by us to make him feel good about himself.[4] This is why praise is best understood as thankfulness and, moreover, a thankfulness that is rooted as much in silent contemplation as in any audible vocalisations. It is a concept that is beautifully captured by the poet W H Auden in his poem "Lullaby" when he declares: "Let your last thinks all be thanks".[5] Note that the word he uses here is not "last words" but "last thinks". It is the thankful heart rather than the praiseful voice which comes closest to experiencing the grace of our Lord. Indeed, Auden's injunction has always struck me as remarkably similar to that of George Herbert, the 17th century British poet and hymn writer, who wrote in his poem "Gratefulness": "Thou that hast given so much to me, give me one thing more: a grateful heart".[6]

The truth of these poetic observations came home to me recently as I was looking at some photographs that I had taken of my second grandson (Oskar) when he was just over a year old. I remembered how he would hold on to me with one hand and race along the room using solid objects like table legs or chairs to propel himself forward. And I remember the first time he managed to stand up on his own without my assistance. He turned around to look at me as if to say 'you see I could do it'. He was instinctively aware that I was behind him, watching over him, and ready to catch him if he fell. We had, of course, strategically put cushions around our tiled floor to break his fall if necessary.

Our protective measure reminded me of Psalm 23 in which the psalmist sings "'he makes me lie down in green pastures" and "restores my soul" (verses 2-3). Phillip Keller in his book "A Shepherd Looks at Psalm 23" gives a helpful insight into the life of a sheep. Sheep, we are told, are built in such a way that if they fall over on their side and then on their back, it is very difficult for them to get up again. They flail their legs in the air, bleat, and cry. After a few hours on their backs, gas begins to collect in their stomachs, the stomach hardens, their air passage is cut off and the sheep eventually suffocate. This is referred to as "a cast down" position. "When a shepherd restores a cast down sheep, he reassures it, massages its legs to restore circulation, gently turns the sheep over and holds it up, so that it can regain its equilibrium".[7]

The actions described by Phillip Keller are exactly what Jesus the Good Shepherd does to his disciples when they are on their backs, feeling discouraged by their failures, angry over their foolish actions or feeling unspiritual. He reassures them of his unfailing love, lifts them up, dusts them down and gives them grace to carry on.

Looking at these photographs of my grandson when he was just a toddler brought home to me the central lesson that I have been trying to impart vis-à-vis the concept of praise and thankfulness. As a toddler, he needed my help but was unable to say "thank you". But it didn't make the slightest bit of difference because I loved him all the same. It was sufficient that the little fellow recognised and welcomed my presence and that I was there for him. The same thing is true of my relationship with God who said to Moses "My presence will go with you and I will give you peace (Exodus 33:14). I know that God doesn't need me to praise him. I know that God doesn't need a single word of thanks from me. But I also know that when I trust God in the way that my grandson trusted me (wordlessly, completely) then I am at peace with myself and the rest of the world.

"From sinking sand, he lifted me; with tender hand, he lifted me; From shades of night to plains of light, O praise His name, He lifted me". (from the chorus of the hymn, "In loving-kindness Jesus came", composed by Charles H Gabriel)

"Even in your old age and with grey hairs, I am he, I am he who will sustain you; I will sustain you and I will rescue you." (Isaiah 46:4)

2. Wrestling with forgiveness

"To live above with saints we love; oh that will be glory. But to live below with saints we know; well that's a different story." (Anon.)

"There is not a righteous man on earth who does what is right and never sins" (Ecclesiastes 7:20)

Each year, as I read again the familiar story of the prodigal son, I am reminded that there is something of the prodigal in all of us because the awareness of human depravity is "the root of perpetual tenderness" (John Newton) and "they who fain would serve Thee best are conscious most of sin within" (the words of an old Presbyterian hymn).

In retirement, names and faces of individuals come to mind. Some fill one with joy, others with lingering resentment or even horror. And there is nothing unscriptural about this. In Romans 16, Paul is full of praise for his faithful supporters and fellow workers but in 2 Timothy 4:14-15 he mentioned one

Alexander the metalworker who did him a "great harm". If you are confronted with insult or antagonism, your first impulse is most likely to respond in kind. Paul responded differently: "The Lord will repay him for what he has done. You too should be on your guard against him, because he strongly opposed our message".

Human minds are not designed to function like a computer with a convenient "delete" key. This partly explains why many Christians continue to feel guilty long after they have sincerely confessed their sin to God, and keep on punishing themselves by saying "if only I hadn't done it". We need to remember that God is infinitely "greater than our hearts" (1 John 3:19-20).

Not long ago, I had a restless night because the day before had ended on a sad note as a result of a cultural disagreement with my closest friend over a matter of no real importance. I was livid at the time and, as so often happens, I said some things of which in retrospect I felt terribly ashamed. I went to bed full of guilt, even after I confessed my sin to God. I was very cross with myself and filled with remorse because I failed to remember that "whoever guards his mouth and his tongue keeps himself from calamity" (Proverbs 21:23).

I woke up in the morning tired and weary; and, as usual, I turned to God's word for comfort. My reading was from 1 John 3:11-20. It was the beginning of verse 20 that caught my attention and made me turn to one of my Bible commentaries for help in understanding the instruction to "set our hearts at rest in God's presence, whenever our hearts condemn us". For I certainly didn't feel comfortable (never mind at rest) in God's presence on that particular morning!

As I pondered on these biblical verses, I arrived at an understanding which has stood me in good stead ever since. More specifically, I realised that the wording of the phrase "whenever our hearts condemn us" suggests that this experience is not unusual for a Christian. On the contrary, as John Stott describes it: "Sometimes the accusations of our conscience – our heart – will be true accusations and sometimes they will be false, inspired by "the accuser of our brethren" (Rev 12:10). In either case, the inner voice is not to overcome us".[8]

In any event, whenever we feel on trial with our heart as the accuser, ourselves as defendant and God as the Judge; we must learn to appeal from our conscience to God who is more knowledgeable and "greater than our hearts". We need honestly to own up before God when we have done wrong (1 John 1:9) but, thereafter, we should not continue to wallow in destructive feelings of guilt and self-flagellation.

More importantly, every time we accept God's forgiveness for our own trespasses, it should serve as a reminder that we, in turn, must exercise forgiveness (or, at least forgetfulness) in respect of those who have wronged us. However, we should not be dismayed if we find ourselves incapable of full and unencumbered forgiveness. Instead, we should remember that only God can truly forgive and not recall our sin (Hebrews 10:17). As observed by the

French philosopher Montaigne, for all human beings, to forgive and forget is a contradiction. You can forget only when you remember; and "there is nothing that so much imprints any thing in our memory as a desire to forget it".[9] His dictums prefigure those of C S Lewis who also commented on the inevitable tension between forgiveness and forgetfulness when he noted that: "to forgive for the moment is not difficult, but to go on forgiving, to forgive the same offence every time it occurs to the memory – that's the real tussle".[10]

The truth of Lewis' words were brought home to me recently when I spotted (albeit at some distance) a former church member that I hadn't seen for many years. When I got home later that day, I heard someone on the radio say, "Happy is the one who forgets what can no longer be changed". After a moment of soul searching I realised that although I *thought* I had forgiven that person for the discord they had brought to our parish church fellowship, I still harboured a deep sense of resentment. In the circumstances, I decided that the best I could do was to "remember to forget".

Reflecting on the value of memory loss, I was reminded of the apocryphal story of a man who complained to his counsellor. "Every time we argue, my wife gets historical". The counsellor tried to correct him by saying "You mean hysterical?". The man snapped back: "No, I mean historical. She drags up everything I've ever done wrong!". And, on a more serious (and bittersweet) note, I also recalled the story of a preacher who asked members of his Bible Study

Group to raise up their hands if they occasionally struggle with forgiveness. Everybody did except the oldest member in her mid-eighties. Asked why, she said: "All the people I used to struggle to forgive have all passed away".

At a theoretical level, I fully agree with Nelson Mandela when he says that "resentment is like drinking poison hoping it will kill your enemies"; and I heartily concur with Edward Herbert when he notes that "he that cannot forgive others breaks the bridge over which he must pass himself; for every man has need to be forgiven".[11] In practice, however, I am all too aware that my attempts to forgive others fall a long way short of the way Christ forgives me. But I am also conscious that if forgetfulness falls short of true forgiveness, it is still a form of letting go. Thankfully, forgetfulness is one of the few activities where old age is correlative with improved performance!

3. Confronting our personal demons

"There is no fear in love. But perfect love drives out fear." (1 John 4:18)

"Do not let your hearts be troubled. Trust in God; trust also in me." (John 14:1)

We all have our personal demons i.e. things we are really scared of and would do everything in our power to avoid. When we are in full time employment, these personal demons are often kept at bay by the psychological barriers of our hectic work schedule. In retirement, however, with time to be and to reflect, we find ourselves in the same position as Shakespeare's Macbeth, with the reality of our "present fears" made worse by "horrible imaginings".

In my case, two of my scariest personal demons are the fear of stroke and memory loss/dementia. I have seen the permanent damage a sudden stroke can inflict overnight on people and the gradual loss of personal dignity that is the handiwork of dementia. And it was the fear of stroke that persuaded me to be put on blood pressure medication at the age of 58. I was told by my GP that I was only marginally at risk but I didn't want to take the chance of becoming a victim of my own inner fear. My dad, shortly after he retired from civil service, drove himself to a clinic for a thorough medical check-up and within 24 hours he was pronounced dead from a massive stroke or heart attack.

The second demon I have to confront is the fear of losing my mind. Little forgetfulness, which is said to be common among the elderly, occasionally now fills me with dread. That is why the best thing said to me recently was by a kind lady at my Diocesan office, who said to me, when I couldn't recall my full previous home address (some 20 year ago) while I was trying to fill a form: "Never mind, Canon Ladipo, you have much to remember; you can complete the form at home and post it back to me."

However, all too often the scariest personal demons are not fears which could materialize in the future but ghosts from our past. "Must go faster" says

Dr Malcolm in the iconic scene from the 1993 movie Jurassic Park movie as he and two other characters flee in a Jeep from a rampaging tyrannosaurus. When the driver looks in the rear mirror, he sees the reptile's jaw-right above the words: "Objects In Mirror May Be Closer Than They Appear". The scene is a masterful combination of intensity and grim humour. But the truth is that the "monsters" from our past often feel like they'll never stop pursuing us. We look in the mirror of our lives and see past mistakes looming right there, threatening to consume us with guilt or shame.

It is the love of God that equips us to let go of our old self, free to look forward in anticipation instead of wallowing backward in fear and regret. My faith in Christ teaches me that it is to no avail to try and confront these personal demons in my own strength. I need God's enabling grace to be at peace with myself.

"Be transformed by the renewing of your mind. Then you will be able to test and approve what God's will is – his good, pleasing and perfect will." (Romans 12:2)

It is deeply comforting to know, like Randy Kilgore, that "God is present in the places where our fears live"[12] and to read again the words of assurance of our Lord that victory over personal demons is possible through the ministry of the Holy Spirit who alone can renew our minds. As the psalmist sings: "My soul finds rest in God alone; my salvation comes from him" (Psalm 62:1).

4. Cultivating Relationships with Family and Close Friends

"Love is the only duty of the present moment." (Jean Pierre de Caussade).[13]

It is possible in old age to be alone without being lonely but very few people can do that for an indefinite period. Loneliness is the most common trigger for depression amongst the elderly. This is because retirement presents new and unexpected psychological challenges. Being cut off from day-to-day interaction with a close-knit church or with work colleagues can feel like a bereavement. To make matters worse, many people find themselves retiring to a location which turns out to be: unsuitable for their immediate and future needs; far from friends and extended family; and with little or no outlet to pursue their interests.

Being together all day long may make the house too small for a retired couple, with each person vying for some space for themselves. There is also plenty of time for a couple to have a close look at each other, without the distraction of children. And the results can be dispiriting and/or comical, depending on one's point of view. For my part, I had to shake my head with wry amusement upon reading an advert for a Church Jumble sale which read: "An opportunity to get rid of something of little use but too precious to throw away – bring your husbands!"

Indeed, it's not until they retire that some couples

realise the enormous battering their marriage relationship had endured while they were in paid employment. By contrast, many couples who worked closely together during their pre-retirement years suddenly find themselves living without a joint purpose. This is especially the case for many retired clergy, or couples who were business partners, because their Church ministry or their shared business had provided them with a platform to work together in partnership. Until retirement, they enjoyed a de-facto "job share" that provided them with a focus around which their married life revolved. Hence when they enter into retirement they may feel like a plank has been taken away from under their feet and they find themselves emotionally in "suspended animation".

I have also experienced multiple cases where a retired couple has approached retirement with different expectations. The husband perhaps hoping it would bring freedom from the "treadmill" of parish or office work; and the possibility of a fresh start in reordering their lives and exploring new opportunities for self-realisation. The wife on the other hand may have hoped that retirement would enable them to put their family first, spending more time with their children and grandchildren and reducing the pace of their frantic lifestyle.

Many retired couples also experience a loss of romantic feelings for each other after years of marriage. Depression, menopause or terminal illness may adversely affect their sexual relationship; and they may need medical help or counselling. For those who, in retirement, discover that their marital relationship has fallen short of being in love, the important thing is to be committed to each other "for better, for worse" and to explore new creative ways of strengthening what is left of their relationship.

"Once the realization is accepted that even between the closest people infinite distances exist, a marvelous living side-by-side can grow up for them, if they succeed in loving the expanse between them, which gives them the possibility of always seeing each other as a whole and before an immense sky." (Rainer Maria Rilke, "Letters to a Young Poet")[14]

In 2011, the number of over-60s in the UK who divorced was 15,275 (up from 10,273 a decade previously), whereupon Relate (the UK's premier marriage counselling service) started to encourage married couples nearing retirement to undergo a "Marriage MOT" together. I remember thinking, at the time, that this was an excellent idea. But if you drive your marriage to the garage and find that a lot of the parts can't be fixed or replaced, what then? Can you still rub along together in old age? Needless to say, each couple has to answer that question for themselves. But whatever arrangement the couple eventually hits upon, it is important for both parties to remember that "Love is holy because it is like grace – the worthiness of its object is never really what matters" (Marilynne Robinson[15]) and that "kindness is in our power even when fondness is not" (Samuel Johnson).

As we enter into our retirement years, we have to

learn to simultaneously embrace and let go of our adult children. It is a lesson that has been taught (and forgotten) down the ages from the time when Socrates addressed this admonition to his peers: "What mean ye fellow citizens that you turn every stone to scrape wealth together and take so little care of your children to whom you must one day relinquish it all". Our children don't have to earn our love. But they should not be smothered by it either. And we must always respect the fact that they are independent persons whose actions are autonomous of ours, whether for good or ill.

We must neither blame each other for the failings of our children nor take undue credit for their success. And, above all, we must never feel ashamed of our adult children but should always remember that the greatest force on earth is not the force of compulsion but the compassion of love. Our loved ones may spurn our appeals, reject our message, oppose our arguments and despise our persons; but they are helpless against our prayers.

By way of illustration, consider the actions of Billy Graham, the renowned evangelist, when his son Franklin Graham (in his rebellious youth) went roaring up to his dad's house on his Harley Davidson motorcycle to ask for money. Dressed in his leathers, dusty and bearded, he burst into his father's living room and walked right into the meeting of Billy Graham's executive board. Without hesitation, Billy Graham identified Franklin as his son. Then he proudly introduced him to every member of the Board. Billy Graham did not apologise for his son's appearance nor show any shame or embarrassment. Franklin wrote later in his autobiography, "Rebel with a Cause", that the love and respect his father gave him that day never left him, even during his rebellious years.

The one group of parents who are real heroes of faith in my book are those who survive the death of their children without lingering bitterness or loss of confidence in God's-loving kindness. They include some Christian friends whose children were born terminally disabled or died young. Their faith and confidence in the loving kindness of God is as strong as that of Job and Abraham. I praise God for them and for the various ways their continuing faithfulness encourages me to trust God more.

At the other end of the spectrum are the couples struggling not with the loss of their beloved children but the unexpected care of new grandchildren. This activity can be a source of joy or conflict. Or both. This is especially true where one party takes great pleasure in child rearing and the other longs for peace and quiet and the preservation of a safe internet distance. In these circumstances, what is crucially important is to be honest with each other and learn to listen, accept and accommodate each other's feelings.

For example, I remember having my first grandson and his parents staying with me for the first time shortly after I retired, when an article appeared in the family section of my daily newspaper. It was entitled "A Children Free Environment" and began with the following sentence: "There comes a time when you want to live without children." It was the story of the Scottish village of Firhall, Britain's first and only childfree village. To buy a house in the village, you have to be forty-five with no dependent child in tow, and you must sign a contract agreeing not to sell property on to those with children.[16] Needless to say, I read it with great interest; but, thankfully the article made me grow into loving my lovely grandchildren all the more!

"Let's choose to live as if this were our last moment on earth by loving more deeply, forgiving more readily, giving more generously, and speaking more kindly. That's how to handle life with care." (Joe Stowell)

In the western world, it is common to find retired couples undertaking some of the work involved in caring for their grandchildren. But it is much less common to find them caring for great nephews and nieces or other members of their wider family network. By contrast, in the developing world, the demands of the extended family can be extremely taxing: economically, spatially and psychologically. Having to cope with endless streams of relatives or friends arriving unannounced – and staying for unspecified periods of time – can be extremely trying, especially for a retired couple. It can sap their energy and deplete their dwindling saving's account. Hence, in their desire to fulfil extended family obligations, even the most hospitable couple must remember that there are two kinds of relatives: the drains and the radiators. The important thing is not to promise your relatives what you know you can't deliver or what is likely to drive a wedge between you and your spouse.

Moreover, whenever the demands of our relatives become insufferable, it is worth remembering Hugh Kingsmill's rueful observation that "Friends are God's apology for relations".[17] In retirement, it is inevitable we lose touch with some friends, which is all the more reason to keep in touch with those we consider our close friends. At a minimum, this involves periodic updating of our address lists, making telephone calls (or sending emails or text messages) to know how they are getting on, and sending greeting cards to mark special occasions. This may sound like a statement of the blindingly obvious but it is surprisingly easy to find that five years have passed since one's last contact with a good friend. A well scheduled approach to correspondence with one's friends may not sound very intimate or spontaneous. But it becomes increasingly necessary the older we get, as our friends become geographically deconcentrated and our own mobility declines.

5. Belonging to a Local Church

"May the Lord make your love increase and overflow for each other and for everyone else, just as ours does for you." (1 Thessalonians 3:12).

For many Christians, church fellowship is a place where they find unconditional love, acceptance and make deep friendships. The church family can be a valuable link to the wider community as well as the source of opportunities to plough back valuable experience gained in paid employment. However, if the newly retired move away from their usual church fellowship they may experience a painful but valuable period of loneliness and of non-belonging. Following the lesson contained in Philippians 2, verse 16 they must learn afresh to "live up to what we have already obtained in Christ".

For anybody seeking guidance on how to fit into a church after retirement, I would counsel them to study the advice contained in Ephesians 4, verses 29-32, which I have quoted in full below:

"Do not let any unwholesome talk come out of your mouths, but only what is helpful for building others up according to their needs, that it may benefit those who listen. And do not grieve the Holy Spirit of God, with whom you were sealed for the day of redemption. Get rid of all bitterness, rage and anger, brawling and slander, along with every form of malice. Be kind and compassionate to one another, forgiving each other, just as in Christ God forgave you."

There is so much good counsel in these four verses, including: the emphasis on being positive role models rather than frivolous attention seekers; the admonition to be mentors rather than trouble makers; and the warning that we should avoid grieving the Holy Spirt by adopting a "know it all" attitude. But when I retired from active duty as an Anglican vicar, it was the fourth verse that held the most important message for me. As retirees we are enjoined to desist from being harshly critical and to focus our energies on being forgiving, encouraging and supportive of young leadership. That said, it is also important to remember that such charitable behaviours may also need to encompass acts of self-forgiveness, especially when the retired member of the clergy unwittingly puts his or her foot into it, by forgetting that they are no longer in charge!

In the course of writing this chapter, I came across a road sign which Mrs Ruth Bell Graham, the wife of Billy Graham, chose to be on her gravestone. It reads: "End of Construction – Thank You for Your Patience". But until we reach the terminal point on our earthly journey, it is important to remember that God is not finished with any of us yet. We still have a lot to learn and a lot to give. The good thing is that God hasn't just left the porch light on for us. He's out on the front porch lovingly watching over us, waiting patiently, until our time is up. To know our Saviour better and to make him better known must remain our aim, leaving behind us a legacy of credible witness to our families.

CHAPTER 4

LEARNING TO COOPERATE WITH THE INEVITABLE

"Man is immortal until his work is done." (Augustine)[1]

Twenty years ago, one cheeky little girl, pointing at me, said to her mother *"That's an old man!"*. The embarrassed mum felt she had to say something and whispered in a low voice: *"He is not quite"*. Two decades later, however, and I think I can confidently declare that I am, indeed, an 'old man'; and my favourite biblical role models have shifted accordingly.

These role models include Simeon, the "righteous and devout" old man who held faith with the revelation vouchsafed to him by the Holy Spirit that "he would not die before he had seen the Lord's Messiah." His reaction upon meeting Jesus is celebrated in the words of the 'Nunc Dimitis' where he declares: *"Lord, now lettest thou thy servant depart in peace according to thy word. For mine eyes have seen thy salvation."*

But as I write this chapter, it is not the celebrated faith of Simeon that most appeals to me but the lesser known example of Anna. In Luke 2:36-38, Anna's story comes immediately after that of Simeon and consists of just three short verses which I have quoted in full below.

"There was also a prophet, Anna, the daughter of Penuel, of the tribe of Asher. She was very old; she had lived with her husband seven years after her marriage, and then was a widow until she was eighty-four. She never left the temple but worshiped night and day, fasting and praying. Coming up to them at that very moment, she gave thanks to God and spoke about the child to all who were looking forward to the redemption of Jerusalem."

At 84 years old, I am now exactly the same age as Anna was at the time she encountered Jesus. And her status as a member of the tribe of Asher, one of the lost tribes of Israel, also resonates with me. For I, too, have spent much of my life living and working in foreign lands. Not surprisingly, the fact that Anna – old and stateless – was amongst the first to testify to the Messiah is a source of great inspiration to me.

Like Simeon, Anna had lived for many years in a state of preparedness for the arrival of the long expected Messiah. And her example reminds us that although the act of waiting tests our patience, it also stretches out our pleasure because it includes the strange joy of anticipation, 'the waiting for Christmas' excitement that we can remember from childhood. In the case of Anna, this state of anticipation lasted a lifetime. She spent her whole life in expectation of the fulfilment of God's redemptive purpose until "her faith was at last changed to sight and her hope to certainty" (to quote the words of Bishop J C Ryle).

I am also drawn to the prophet Anna because she reminds me of the English anchoress, Julian of Norwich. As described in her 14th century manuscript, entitled 'Revelations of Devine Love', she prayed for God's "gifts" of 'three wounds" to enable her to understand Christ's passion, namely: the wounds of true contrition; the wounds of genuine compassion; and the wounds of sincere longing for God.

Later, she would write the following:

"God is true rest. It is his will that we should know him and his pleasure that we should rest in him. God of your goodness give me yourself, for you are sufficient for me. I cannot ask anything less to be worthy of you. If I were to ask less, I should always be in want".[2]

Taking, as my inspiration, the twin examples of Anna of Jerusalem and Julian of Norwich, I hope to use this final chapter to illustrate how the subjective experience of the ageing process depends, at a very fundamental level, on one's spiritual perspective. More specifically, I will outline how the study of God's word can transform our outlook with regard to each of the following experiences:

i. *Senescence*: From a weakening of the body to a re-clothing of the soul.

ii. *Pain*: From groaning with shame to groaning with gratitude, solidarity and expectation.
iii. *Boredom*: From impatience to immersion in the present.
iv. *Mountain climbing*: From paralysis to taking one step at a time.
v. *Death*: From angry resistance to graceful cooperation.

In the sections that follow, I will briefly elaborate on each of these shifts in perspective.

1. Senescence: From a weakening of the body to a re-clothing of the soul

"I have never met a man who has given me as much trouble as myself." (Dwight L Moody)

"We sicken before we die so that we will be weaned from our body." (J M Coetzee)[3]

To mark her 75th birthday Maya Angelou proceeded to sing the final verse of her poem 'On Ageing':

"I'm the same person I was back then
A little less hair, a little less chin,
A lot less lungs and much less wind.
But ain't I lucky I can still breathe in."[4]

The older we are the more likely it is that our bodies will let us down. In my own case, I suffer from all the maladies listed by Maya Angelou and plenty of others she didn't mention, including erratic waterworks. This is why I appreciate the tale told by John Mortimer of a trip he took while on a speaking tour in the US. He was met at Miami Airport by a judge in a black stretch limo wearing a dinner jacket. As they were crossing the Everglades he told the judge (called "Mr Sanchez") that he needed to pee rather urgently. He was told there was a nice restaurant with "a clean restroom twenty miles ahead". Mortimer replied, "Mr. Sanchez, twenty miles is of no interest to me, if you wouldn't mind stopping for 3 minutes I'll get out here".

The road looked empty, the limo purred to a stop, and he stepped out on the grass edge. Just before he got down to business he asked Mr. Sanchez, "what are those black things that look like a pile of spare tires by the side of the road up there?" "Those, sir," Mr. Sanchez said as calmly as ever, "are alligators". In response, Mortimer "pulled up the zip and dived back into the car, ready to face a painful twenty-mile drive to the restroom"[5].

The late, left-wing Labour MP Tony Benn also recounts an experience that was less painful but no less risible and humiliating. While driving his car over Vauxhall Bridge in London, his bladder began to play up. As he puts it: "It was clear I wouldn't make it home in time. So, I got out of the car, opened the hood and, well, did what I needed to do." And just when he thought he'd got away with it, he was accosted by a passer-by who said, "I think I know your problem. Your radiator is leaking".[6]

I laugh when I read these stories because I know, all too well, the sense of panic that the narrators experienced. Indeed, having lived in London for many decades, I am aware that public toilets have become a very scarce commodity. But London is not the only capital city in which I have suffered the indignity of being caught short. A few years ago, I found myself in a familiar predicament, right in the middle of a horrendous traffic jam in the very centre of Abuja, Nigeria's federal capital.

We were holed up in the same spot for half an hour, by which time I had become increasingly desperate to go to the loo. Our location was less than half a mile from our destination (a city centre hotel). But, fearful of wetting my trousers, I got out of the car, dodged my way across two lanes of traffic and eventually reached the back of an outer high wall of the hotel. There was hardly anybody passing by. So, by then, close to bursting, I asked a man walking towards me where the nearest toilet could be found. Without even looking at my contorted face, he said: "Anywhere; this is a free country". So, against the wall I hurriedly did what I had to do! On my way back to locate my driver I began to laugh saying to myself: "It's good to be back home in the land of the free". Nor was it difficult to locate my driver; he was still exactly where I had left him!

A good sense of humour can certainly help to alleviate the physical suffering and social indignities that assail us in retirement and old age. But the power to lift a man out of his suffering in the face of decay and death does not come from within himself; it comes from God:

"Therefore we do not lose heart. Though outwardly we are wasting away, yet inwardly we are being renewed day by day. For our light and momentary troubles are achieving for us an eternal glory that far outweighs them all." (2 Cor 4:16-17)

Yes, my muscles may ache and my joints may hurt and my bladder may have a life of its own. But Paul's letters to the Corinthians remind us that the failings of a decrepit body that lamentably refuses to oblige are not accidental. To put it in modern computer programming jargon, our bodies' built-in senescence is not a 'defect' or a 'flaw'. On the contrary, it is an essential feature of God's plan:

"God who said, 'Let light shine out of darkness', made his light shine in our hearts to give us the light of the knowledge of God's glory displayed in the face of Christ. But we have this treasure in jars of clay to show that this all-surpassing power is from God and not from us." (2 Cor 4:6-7).

"We always carry around in our body the death of Jesus, so that the life of Jesus may also be revealed in our body. For we who are alive are always being given over to death for Jesus' sake, so that his life may also be revealed in our mortal body." (2 Cor 4:10-11).

Once we start to view things from this perspective, we begin to appreciate that our physical decrepitude is best seen not as a failure to be regretted but as an essential process of refinement. Our senescence is the method by which the crude clay of our bodies is removed so that God's light, "which shines in our hearts", can be seen all the more brightly. And the closer we come to death, the more we seek to shed our earthly clothing and become re-clothed in God's love.

"For we know that if the earthly tent we live in is destroyed, we have a building from God, an eternal house in heaven, not built by human hands. Meanwhile we groan, longing to be clothed instead with our heavenly dwelling, because when we are clothed, we will not be found naked. For while we are in this tent, we groan and are burdened, because we do not wish to be unclothed but to be clothed instead with our heavenly dwelling, so that what is mortal may be swallowed up by life." (2 Cor 5:1-4).

2. Pain: From groaning with shame to groaning with gratitude, solidarity and expectation

"Heaven knows we need never be ashamed of our tears, for they are rain upon the blinding dust of earth, overlying our hard hearts. I was better after I had cried, than before – more sorry, more aware of my own ingratitude, more gentle." (Charles Dickens)[7]

Pains of all kinds (back, neck, hip, knee), heartache (literal and metaphorical), and memory loss are all part of getting older. Consequently, for many people, old age is not the mellow and gentle phase of life conjured up by the phrase the 'golden years'. On the contrary, it is a period in which the daily soundtrack of our lives is punctuated every few minutes by moans and groans of various durations, timbre and intensity.

But groaning has been given a very bad press in a generation that thrives on hyper activity and a church that appears to have lost sight of a biblical theology of suffering.

"Stop groaning and get on with it", a father barks at his grown-up son. And yet, never once in my hospital visiting did I come across a dying patient who did not groan, no matter how very faintly.

In retirement, groaning becomes an involuntary activity of old age. As Larry Crabb puts it, in his book 'Inside Out': the truth is that "we either groan or pretend we don't."[8] Yet one of the problems with modern Christianity is that it tries, all too often, to deny this truth. We are cruelly exhorted to stop groaning; but these exhortations simply add to our distress by making us ashamed of our feelings.

Instead of being ashamed of our groans and attempting to stifle them, we need to convert them into a vital part of the process by which we learn to cooperate with our inevitable physical deterioration. And what are the keys to this conversion?

The first and most important key is gratitude. It is only by looking back with gratitude over years of God's faithfulness that we can turn our groans of shame into groans of gratitude. This is the experience of the Psalmist when the "cords of death" entangle him, the "anguish of the grave" comes upon him and he is "overcome with trouble and sorrow". He groans and cries out to heaven: "O Lord save me!" (Psalm 116:3-4). But it is only when he remembers God's bountifulness to him over the years that his suffering is quieted and he can say: "Be at rest once more, O my soul, for the Lord has been good to you" (Psalm 116:7).

The second key is the remembrance that involuntary groaning is not a lonely exercise. On the contrary, when we groan with pain or humiliation or loneliness, we are in fact in the company of the Holy Spirit who "intercedes for us with groans that words cannot express in accordance with God's will" (Romans 8:26-27).

The third key is one that we encountered in the preceding section, namely the substitution of anxiety for expectation. As we have already seen in 2 Cor 5:1-4, Paul describes our groans as expressions of our longing to be "clothed" with our "heavenly dwelling".

This idea is further articulated in Paul's letter to the Romans where he notes that:

"The whole creation has been groaning as in the pains of childbirth right up to the present time. Not only so, but we ourselves, who have the first fruits of the Spirit, groan inwardly as we wait eagerly for our adoption to sonship, the redemption of our bodies." (Romans 8:22-23)

3. Boredom: From killing time to living in time

"We have become too much afraid of boredom and we do ourselves no favours by living a life continually in flight from it." (Revd. Giles Fraser)[9]

"The killing of time is the worst of murders." (Daniel Defoe)[10]

The debate over the role boredom plays in human well-being became especially salient during the global coronavirus lockdown. The bulk of this debate consisted of personal stories. My daily paper, for example, ran numerous first person articles about the 'stifling' effect of being stuck at home with nothing 'interesting' to do. But it also gave plenty of column inches to writers championing the 'liberating' effects of the imposed solitude and 'downtime'.

Every now and again, the authors of these articles would seek to buttress their views on the merits and demerits of boredom by wheeling out their favourite philosophical spokespersons. We would be told, for example, that Schopenhauer was "arguably the first Western philosopher to take boredom seriously as one of the primary miseries of humankind". Or, conversely, we would be pointed in the direction of Nietzsche whose views on the topic of boredom included the following: "He who fortifies himself completely against boredom fortifies himself against himself too. He will never drink the most powerful elixir from his own innermost spring"[11].

My own views on the subject of boredom lean

towards those of Nietzsche but are not quite as radical as those of Robert Heinlein, who once opined that: "Progress isn't made by early risers. It's made by lazy and bored people trying to find easier ways of doing something".[12] Unlike Heinlein, I'm still a believer in the progressive power of hard work and early morning starts. But I'm equally convinced that a spot of mid-afternoon tedium helps to stimulate one's creative juices.

For many retirees, however, debates over the merits and demerits of boredom are not an academic exercise to be enjoyed over a convivial post-pandemic glass of wine. On the contrary, the experience of boredom is a daily challenge that can prove deeply de-energising and demoralising. This is especially true in an era where the word "time" has become the most often used noun in the English language and "doing nothing" is a denigrated and devalued activity.

In this context, it is helpful to remind ourselves of the biblical perspective on 'time management' that is articulated in the following injunction:

"Be very careful, then, how you live – not as unwise but as wise, making the most of every opportunity, because the days are evil. Therefore, do not be foolish, but understand what the Lord's will is. Do not get drunk on wine, which leads to debauchery. Instead, be filled with the Spirit, speaking to one another with psalms, hymns, and songs from the Spirit. Sing and make music from your heart to the Lord, always giving thanks to God the Father for everything, in the name of our Lord Jesus Christ." (Ephesians 5:15-20)

In this passage from Paul's letter to the Ephesians, he urges us not to waste our time but to make use of "every opportunity". But he means this in a very pre-modern sense. He is not asking us to busy ourselves with remunerative 'work' or egocentric projects of 'self-improvement' or 'self-development'. No, on the contrary, his first injunction is that we use our time to be filled with the Holy Spirit and to connect with other people, to speak with them and sing with them.

I was reminded of this passage from Ephesians when I met an elderly lady in church during a youth programme presentation. It was noisy, boisterous, inordinate and full of spontaneous laughter and hand clapping. Half way through the presentation, my new acquaintance helped herself to some 'polo' mints and offered me some too. When I politely declined, she said by way of explanation: "I only eat these when I am bored". At that moment, her boredom – without her even knowing - was a gift from the Holy Spirit because it prompted her to connect with another human being and to make that person laugh and smile. Moreover, as the service progressed, like the rest of the congregation, she sang hymns and gave thanks to God; and unless I'm very much mistaken, she was a good deal more cheerful at the end of the service than she had been at the beginning.

Moreover, in my reading of Paul's advice to the Ephesians, boredom is a multivalent gift from the Holy Spirit. Not only does boredom serve as a prompt for human connection and human creativity but it can also be transformed into an opportunity to appreciate God's bountifulness and "give thanks to

God for everything".

Paul's admonition is beautifully illustrated in a story that I came across some years ago. Whilst I can't vouch for the literal truth of this story, its metaphorical truth is something that has resonated with me ever since I heard it. It is the tale of a wealthy industrialist who found a poor fisherman sitting lazily beside his boat.

"Why are you not out fishing?", asked the industrialist.

"Because I've caught enough fish for today," replied the fisherman.

"Why don't you catch more fish than you need?", the rich man asked.

"What would I do with them?", replied the fisherman.

"You could earn more money and have a fleet of boats and be rich like me", the rich man explained.

The fisherman asked, "Then what would I do?"

"You could sit down and enjoy life", said the rich man.

"What do you think I'm doing now?", asked the fisherman as he looked placidly at the sea.

When last did you look placidly around the beauty of God's wonderful creation?

4. Mountain climbing: From paralysis to taking one step at a time

"Today is the tomorrow I worried about yesterday." (Sam Taylor-Wood)[13]

In my seminars, I like to tell the story of a couple that went jogging every Saturday morning. The route they followed ended on a steep hill; and every time they approached it the husband would say to his wife "Are you ready for the hill, my dear?". Until, one day, the wife blurted out: "Will you please stop saying that?! You make it sound as if I am climbing Mount Everest and that discourages me".

Difficult things can become impossible to handle properly if we think we have to be completely ready for the uphill task. In my own case, I am conscious that I live in a world of increasing technological complexity and tasks that appear 'simple' and intuitive to my grandchildren (e.g. participating in a zoom meeting) actually comprise multiple steps, none of which seem remotely intuitive to me. The result, all too often, is that a state of paralysis threatens to overcome me until I remember to just take things 'one step at a time'.

Moreover, for many retirees, the difficulties encountered in navigating modern technology are the least of the problems they have to deal with because almost *every* task becomes harder the older one gets. Filing tax returns, finding an emergency plumber, travelling across the city on public transport, navigating one's way through a public hospital, trying to access one's pension entitlements, joining a gym, recovering from a bereavement. Any one of these activities can seem like a Herculean exercise. And, if we're honest, what often makes these tasks seem all the more impossible is the very fact that they seem so easy for 'other' people.

This is why humility is an essential piece of climbing gear for any mountaineering senior citizen. It is the same humility that was required of Moses during the exodus from Egypt. What would have happened if Moses had worried about how he was going to feed the thousands of people of Israel who followed him into the wilderness? Paralysis would have occurred and he would never have taken that first step forwards. This is why God unambiguously told Moses to take the journey one step at a time.

"I will rain down bread from heaven for you. The people are to go out each day and gather enough for that day. In this way I will test them and see whether they will follow my instructions." (Exodus 16:4)

Whenever I keep wondering how God is going to get me out of what looks like an impossible situation, I have to remind myself again and again that God's grace is sufficient for my need and that his power is made perfect in my weakness. Every hill in life is too high if we think we must climb it all at once. But no hill is insurmountable if we follow God's instructions and take one step at a time.

In his first epistle, Peter makes the same point when he observes that the best antidote for fear and discouragement is "to cast your care and anxieties on God because he cares for you". However, in the preceding sentence, Peter also reminds us that this antidote is only accessible through humility: "Humble yourselves, therefore, under God's mighty hand, that he may lift you up in due time" (1 Peter 5:6-7). When faced with trials and tribulations that threaten to overwhelm us, we have to let go of our anxiety, our anger and our impatient resistance to the mysterious leading of God. We have to enter into the state of humility and trust that is so wonderfully described in this verse by John Newman (which is rarely sung nowadays):

"Lead kindly Light, amid the encircling gloom
lead Thou me on
The night is dark, and I am far from home
lead Thou me on
Keep Thou my feet, I do not ask to see
the distant scene, one step is enough for me."

Our Lord, by his own example, also showed us that this same humility can carry us forward through any journey, no matter how terrifying and unbearable. When Jesus wandered in the wilderness for forty days without food he showed us how to withstand the most extreme temptations. Instead of trying to draw on his own strength, Jesus put all his trust in God and humbly observed: "It is written: Man shall not live on bread alone" (Luke 4:1-11). And in his final hour on the cross, when his work of redemption was accomplished, Jesus marked his final step with the simple observation that: "It is finished" (John 19:30).

5. Death: From angry resistance to graceful cooperation

I remember when I was a young man, every formal invitation card used to end with "DV" (Deo Volente) which in Latin means "God willing". But if this tradition has long since fallen into abeyance, the need to plan with God in mind remains as strong as it has ever been. Indeed, in our secular age, it is all the more important that we listen to the admonitions of James the Apostle when he says:

"Now listen, you who say, 'Today or tomorrow we will go to this or that city, spend a year there, carry on business and make money.' Why, you do not even know what will happen tomorrow. What is your life? You are a mist that appears for a little while and then vanishes. Instead, you ought to say, 'If it is the Lord's will, we will live and do this or that'." (James 4:13-15)

For, on the night before his death, Jesus himself taught us how to submit to God's will rather than our own futile desires. That night, Jesus went as usual to the Mount of Olives and his disciples followed him. But upon reaching the place, Luke tells us that:

"He withdrew about a stone's throw beyond them, knelt down and prayed, 'Father, if you are willing, take this cup from me; yet not my will, but yours be done.' An angel from heaven appeared to him and strengthened him. And being in anguish,

he prayed more earnestly, and his sweat was like drops of blood falling to the ground." (Luke 22:41-44)

It is instructive to note that Christ's prayer was a prayer of total submission to the will of God. Like all of us, Jesus was scared of the process of dying and was fearful of the bitter "cup" that lay ahead of him. But instead of surrendering to anger and resentment, he put all his faith in God: "yet not my will but yours be done". And God, in turn, reciprocated and sent him an angel to strengthen him.

Moreover, the subsequent two verses in Luke's account of Christ's last night on the Mount of Olives are also worth studying. For they tell us that after exhausting himself in prayer and humble submission, Jesus rose and went back to the disciples and found them asleep, "exhausted from sorrow". "Why are you sleeping?" he asked them. "Get up and pray so that you will not fall into temptation" (Luke 22:45-56).

What we see in these verses is that a humble acceptance of the inevitability of death can help us to focus our attention on the needs of others, especially those of our family and close friends. But, all too often, people leave this reckoning with the inevitable until a point where it is too late. Not only have they given themselves insufficient time to be fortified with God's love, but they have also neglected to specify the medical directives that can help both them and their loved ones.

These medical directives include specific, *ex-ante,* written instructions that help medical staff address the following questions when faced with patients

suffering from terminal illness:
  i. *Do you want to be resuscitated if your heart stops?*
  ii. *Do you want aggressive treatments such as intubation and mechanical ventilation?*
  iii. *Do you want antibiotics?*
  iv. *Do you want tube or intravenous feeding if you can't eat on your own?*

In recent years, modern medical sciences have made it possible to keep people alive for long stretches of time even if they have lost all consciousness and can only survive when hooked up to their 'life support' machines. And, in the absence of pre-formulated medical directives, the decision as to when to switch off a life-support machine typically rests with the patient's family under advice from the doctor in charge. All too often this places a terrible psychological burden on the patient's loved ones and, for that matter, on the patient's medical staff. Our children, grandchildren, friends and our community at large will all be affected by our death. It is, therefore, incumbent upon us to ensure that we plan accordingly and with a view to minimising the stress that we place upon them, whether financial, organisational or psychological.

However, from a Christian perspective, there is another, more compelling, reason to ensure that we have crafted a legally, binding, 'advanced medical directive', namely the prospect of eternal life. Indeed, I can think of no better argument in favour of such advanced instructions than the concluding paragraph to the medical directive written by the Revd. John

Stott, the renowned preacher and Bible expositor.

Stott's medical directive concludes as follows:

"I do not wish my life to be artificially prolonged if thereby I am left in a terminal or vegetative state. The reason I do not wish to cling to life is that I have a living hope of a yet more glorious life beyond death; I do not wish to be unnecessarily hindered from inheriting it."[14]

John Stott's faith, as exhibited in the words above, not only reminds us that death is inevitable but also encourages us to hold on firmly and confidently to the promise of eternal life, as Paul did in Philippians 1:20-21, when he declared:

"I eagerly expect and hope that I will in no way be ashamed, but will have sufficient courage so that now as always Christ will be exalted in my body, whether by life or by death. For to me, to live is Christ and to die is gain."

Like John Stott, we must always be mindful of the spiritual example that we set our loved ones. For, like it or not, the way in which we resist or cooperate with the inevitable will have a lasting and powerful impact on those around us.

I was reminded of this some years ago, when I was greatly blessed to be by the bedside of the very man who led me to Christ. It was a few hours before he died and what I saw that afternoon was a breathless Tony Wilmot at peace in the Lord. I felt humbled to be asked to pray what, later that day, turned out to be an advance prayer of committal. For, later that same night, when no one was around, Uncle Tony sneaked out to heaven.

Uncle Tony's sublime equanimity in the face of death was founded on a deep and unwavering faith in the promises of our Lord. It was a faith every bit as strong as that possessed by the 19th century American evangelist, D L Moody, when he confidently declared: "Some day you will read in the papers that D. L. Moody, of East Northfield, is dead. Don't you believe a word of it! At that moment I shall be more alive than I am now. I shall have gone up higher, that is all; out of this old clay tenement into a house that is immortal."[15]

When my time eventually comes, I hope that I will be able to cooperate with the inevitable with a like degree of faith, humility and joyful anticipation. And, until the Lord calls me home, I will cleave to this prayer by Richard of Chichester:

"Thanks be to Thee, my Lord Jesus Christ,
For all the benefits that Thou hast given me,
For all the pains and insults that Thou hast borne for me;
O merciful Redeemer, Friend and Brother,
May I know Thee more clearly,
love thee more dearly, and follow thee more nearly."[16]

EPILOGUE

In Chapter 3 of this book, I drew a parallel between the poem "Lullaby" by the 20th century poet, W H Auden, and the poem "Gratefulness" by the 17th century poet and hymn writer, George Herbert. In this epilogue, I would like to draw a different parallel, this time between Herbert's poem "Life" and Psalm 90:5-6.

Let's begin with the Psalm:

"You sweep men away in the sleep of death,
they are like the new grass of the morning,
though in the morning it springs up,
by evening it is dry and withered."

And now hear its echo in Herbert's poem:

"I made a posy, while the day ran by:
'Here will I smell my remnant out, and tie
*   My life within this band.'*
But Time did beckon to the flowers, and they
By noon most cunningly did steal away,
*   And withered in my hand.*

My hand was next to them, and then my heart;
I took, without more thinking, in good part
                Time's gentle admonition;
Who did so sweetly death's sad taste convey,
Making my mind to smell my fatal day,
                Yet, sug'ring the suspicion.

Farewell dear flowers, sweetly your time ye spent,
Fit, while ye lived, for smell or ornament,
                And after death for cures.
I follow straight without complaints or grief,
Since, if my scent be good, I care not if
                It be as short as yours."[1]

I treasure this poem not just because of its evocative portrayal of the evanescence of human life but for two other reasons. Firstly, the poem provides a powerful reminder that what matters, in the end, is not the length but the quality of our time on earth – we all have *'time enough'* to make a difference. Secondly, the poem's biblical echoes include both the poetry of the Psalmist and the prose of Saint Paul. Herbert's willingness to "follow straight without complaints or grief" is a mirror of the confidence displayed by Paul when he declared that "For me, to live is Christ and to die is gain" (Philippians 1:21).

For me too, without Christ I am not ready to die. But with faith in Christ, I have every reason to stay alive until my time is up.

What about you?!

NOTES

Ch 1: Life Gets Shorter by the Day

[1] Spalding Grey quoted in the documentary *And Everything Is Going Fine*, directed by Steven Soderbergh, 2010.

[2] Toni Morrison quoted in Ellen Brown, "Writing is Third Career for Morrison", *The Cincinnati Enquirer*, 27 September 1981.

[3] Billy Graham, *Nearing Home: Life, Faith, and Finishing Well*, Thomas Nelson, 2011.

[4] Penelope Lively, "So this is old age", *The Guardian*, 5 October 2013.

[5] Atul Gawande, "Letting Go", *The New Yorker*, 2 Aug 2010.

[6] Guy Brown, *The Living End : The Future of Death, Aging and Immortality*, Macmillan, 2008.

[7] James Wilsdon, "The Way to Go", *Financial Times*, 22 February 2008.

[8] Aubrey de Grey quoted in Elmo Keep, "Can Human Mortality Really Be Hacked?", *Smithsonian Magazine*, June 2017.

[9] Ibid.

[10] Quoted in Sid Kirchheimer, "Anti-Aging Snake Oil", *AARP Bull. Today*, 9 November 2005.

[11] Albert Einstein quoted in David P. Sentner, "Would Take Three Days To Make Simple Explanation Of Theories, Says Einstein", *Clearfield Progress*, 12 December 1930.

[12] Jenny Agutter quoted in Rosanna Greenstreet, "Q&A", *The Guardian*, 13 January 2018.

[13] Leon Trotsky, *Diary in Exile*, Faber & Faber, 1959.

[14] Rowan Williams, *Being Human: Bodies, Minds, Persons*, SPCK Publishing, 2018.

[15] Dmitri Shostakovich, quoted in Julian Barnes, *Nothing to be Frightened Of*, Vintage, 2009.

[16] Joseph Epstein, "Kid Turns 70", *The Weekly Standard*, 29 January 2007.

[17] Thomas à Kempis, *The Imitation of Christ*, Penguin, 2013.

[18] Dylan Thomas, "Do not go gentle into that good night", *The Collected Poems of Dylan Thomas*, edited by John Goodby, Weidenfeld & Nicolson, 2014.

[19] Robert Frost, "The Death of the Hired Man", *The Collected Poems*, Vintage Classics, 2013.

[20] Francis Thompson, "The Hound of Heaven", *The Hound of Heaven and other Poems*, International Pocket Library, 2000.

[21] Charles Spurgeon, "Help from on High", *The Complete Works of C. H. Spurgeon*, Delmarva Publications, 2013.

Ch 2: Retirement is a New Adventure

[1] Judith Stern quoted in Bennett Cerf, *The Laugh's on Me*, Doubleday, 1959.

[2] Susan Ertz, *Anger in the Sky*, Hodder & Stoughton, 1948.

[3] Maurice Chevalier quoted in Charles D. Rice, "Meet the most quotable quotes", *Los Angeles Times*, 15 May 1960.

[4] William James, *The Principles of Psychology,* Vol. I, Henry Holt & Co, 1890.

[5] Meike Ziervogel, *Clara's Daughter*, Salt Publishing, 2014.

[6] Arthur Schopenhauer, *Parerga and Paralipomena*, Vol. I, Cambridge University Press, 2014.

[7] William H. Thomas, *What Are Old People For? How Elders Will Save the World*, Vanderwyk & Burnham, 2004.

[8] Phillip Larkin, "The Old Fools", *Phillip Larkin: Collected Poems*, edited by Anthony Thwaite, Faber & Faber, 2003.

[9] Michael Banner, *The Ethics of Everyday Life*, Oxford University Press, 2014.

[10] Mary Warnock and Elisabeth Macdonald, *Easeful Death: Is There a Case for Assisted Dying?*, Oxford University Press, 2009.

[11] George Pitcher, *A Time to Live: The Case Against Euthanasia and Assisted Suicide*, Monarch Books, 2010.

[12] Titus Lucretius Carus, *On the Nature of Things,* translated by Cyril Bailey, Ulan Press, 2012.

[13] Drue Heinz quoted in Charles Moore, "The Spectator's Notes", *The Spectator*, 19 July 2018.

[14] Mark Twain, *A Connecticut Yankee in King Arthur's Court*, Harper & Brothers Publishers, New York, 1889.

[15] Rowan Williams, *Being Human: Bodies, Minds, Persons*, SPCK Publishing, 2018.

[16] Desmond Tutu, *Made for Goodness*, Rider, 2012.

[17] Dame Julian of Norwich quoted in Ibid.

[18] Oprah Winfrey quoted in Ibid.

[19] This quotation is often attributed to Winston Churchill or Abraham Lincoln. But the author has yet to find any official record thereof.

[20] Alec Guinness, *A Positively Final Appearance*, Penguin, 2000.

[21] Epictetus, "The Enchiridion", in *Discourses and Selected Writings*, translated and edited by Robert Dobbin, 2008.

[22] This quotation has been attributed to multiple people, mostly commonly the Scottish physician and novelist, A J Cronin.

[23] This is another quotation whose provenance is doubtful, albeit it is often attributed to Ingrid Bergman.

[24] Rhena Taylor, quoted in her obituary, *Crosslinks Magazine*, 13 October 2013.

Ch 3: Deepening of Loving Relationships

[1] This quotation has been attributed to both Jeanne Moreau and Anaïs Nin.

[2] Quoted in Garry Apgar and Edward Langille, *The Quotable Voltaire*, Rutgers University Press, 2021.

[3] Marilynne Robinson, *Home*, Virago, 2008.

[4] C.S. Lewis, *Reflections on the Psalms*, HarperOne, 2017.

[5] W.H. Auden, "Lullaby", *W.H. Auden: Collected Poems*, edited by Edward Mendelson, Faber & Faber, 1994.

[6] George Herbert, "Gratefulness", *George Herbert: The Complete Poetry*, edited by John Drury, Penguin, 2015.

[7] Phillip Keller, *A Shepherd Looks at Psalm 23*, Inspiro, 2005.

[8] John Stott, *Epistles of John*, Inter-Varsity Press, July 1964.

[9] Michel de Montaigne, *The Complete Essays*, Penguin 1993.

[10] C.S. Lewis, *Letters to Malcolm: Chiefly on Prayer*, Mariner Books, 2002.

[11] Edward Herbert, *The Autobiography of Edward, Lord Herbert of Cherbury*, edited by Sidney L. Lee, Cambridge University Press, 2013.

[12] Randy Kilgore, quoted in *Our Daily Bread*, Ministérios Pão Diário, 2016.

[13] Jean-Pierre De Caussade, *The Sacrament of the Present Moment*, HarperOne, 1989.

[14] Rainer Maria Rilke, *Letters to a Young Poet*, Penguin, 2016.

[15] Marilynne Robinson, *Gilead*, Virago, 2004.

[16] Julie Bindel, "There comes a time when you want to live without children", *The Guardian*, 8 April 2006.

[17] Hugh Kingsmill quoted in Michael Holroyd, *Best of Hugh Kingsmill*, Victor Gollancz, 1970.

Ch 4: Learning to Cooperate with the Inevitable

[1] This is not a verbatim quote from Augustine but, rather, a paraphrasing of one of the core messages contained in his magnum opus, *The City of God*, edited by G.R. Evans, Penguin, 2003.

[2] Julian of Norwich, *Revelations of Divine Love*, translated by Elizabeth Spearing, Penguin, 1998.

[3] J.M. Coetzee, *Age of Iron*, Penguin, 2010.

[4] Maya Angelou, "On Ageing", *And Still I Rise*, Virago, 1986.

[5] John Mortimer, *The Summer of a Dormouse*, Penguin, 2001.

[6] Quoted in Jack Malvern, "People: Sir David Attenborough; Alan Bennett; Tony Benn; Boy George", *The Times*, 22 January 2009.

[7] Charles Dickens, *Great Expectations*, Penguin, 2004.

[8] Larry Crabb, *Inside Out*, NavPress, 2013.

[9] Giles Fraser, "Spiritually, We Do Ourselves No Favours Constantly Trying To Avoid Boredom", *The Guardian*, 23 August 2013.

[10] Daniel Defoe quoted in Sandi Toksvig, *Peas & Queues: The Minefield of Modern Manners*, Profile Books, 2013.

[11] The Schopenhauer and Nietzsche quotations can both be found in Steven Poole's review of "Out of My Skull" by James Danckert and John D Eastwood, *The Guardian*, 28 May, 2020.

[12] Robert Heinlein, *Time Enough For Love*, Penguin, 1973.

[13] Sam Taylor-Wood quoted in Rosanna Greenstreet, "Q&A", *The Guardian*, 15 Nov 2008.

[14] Quoted by John Stott's biographer, Bishop Dudley-Smith, at his Memorial Service at St. Paul's Cathedral, London, on 13 April 3012.

[15] William Revell Moody, *D.L. Moody*, Fleming H. Revell, 1900.

[16] "Acts and Other Devotions", Prayer 48, *The Churchman's Prayer Manual*, G.R. Bullock-Webster, 1913.

Epilogue

[1] George Herbert, "Life", *George Herbert: The Complete Poetry*, edited by John Drury, Penguin, 2015

ABOUT THE AUTHOR

Revd. Canon Yemi Ladipo was born and raised in Ibadan, Nigeria, in 1937. In 1961 he came to England to prepare for a career in public administration. But his plans changed when he felt God's call to the ministry. He then trained at Clifton Theological College, Bristol and was ordained in the Anglican Communion at Lichfield Cathedral in 1966. Three years later, in 1969, he and his wife, Sue, returned to Nigeria to found the Great Commission Movement of Nigeria ("GCMN"). Alongside his work at GCMN, Yemi also spent four years as the Vicar of St. Piran's Church in Jos. In 1982, he moved to Kenya upon his appointment as African Field Director for Campus Crusade for Christ. During his stay in Kenya, he served as honorary priest at All Saint's Cathedral, Nairobi.

In 1984, Yemi and his family returned to the UK where his parochial ministry included the vicarships of three parish churches: St Stephen's, Canonbury; St. Paul's, Herne Hill; and St. Michael's, South Malling. In addition to his parish work, Yemi also spent time as the Secretary for International Mission at BCMS Crosslinks, where his lectures and publications on the need for "reciprocal partnerships" in world mission helped guide the work of a younger generation of Christian leaders. During this time, Yemi also served on the Council of the London Institute of Contemporary Christianity and the Council of All Nations Christian College.

Upon his retirement from full-time parochial service in 2002, Yemi continued his commitment to international mission through his participation in the Lee Abbey Council and the Lee Abbey International Students Club Board. He remains actively involved in his local churches and travels regularly to Nigeria to provide mentorship and support for the GCMN fellowship.

Printed in Great Britain
by Amazon